"Interfere, Restrict, Control"

Restraints on Freedom of Association in Bahrain

Human Rights Watch is dedicated to protecting the human rights of people around the world. We stand with victims and activists to prevent discrimination, to uphold political freedom, to protect people from inhumane conduct in wartime, and to bring offenders to justice. We investigate and expose human rights violations and hold abusers accountable. We challenge governments and those who hold power to end abusive practices and respect international human rights law. We enlist the public and the international community to support the cause of human rights for all.

Human Rights Watch is an international organization with staff in more than 40 countries, and offices in Amsterdam, Beirut, Berlin, Brussels, Chicago, Geneva, Goma, Johannesburg, London, Los Angeles, Moscow, Nairobi, New York, Paris, San Francisco, Tokyo, Toronto, Tunis, Washington DC, and Zurich.

For more information, please visit our website: http://www.hrw.org

JUNE 2013

ISBN: 978-1-62313-0299

"Interfere, Restrict, Control"

Restraints on Freedom of Association in Bahrain

Summary

Civic engagement and political activism have long played an important role in Bahrain, a Gulf nation 30 kilometers off the coast of Saudi Arabia that is home to some 1.2 million people.

Since independence from Britain in 1971, social, cultural, and sports clubs, as well as civil and professional organizations, have been pivotal in shaping political debate. With political groups of any sort prohibited until 2001, nongovernmental organizations (NGOs) have often served as forums for discussing social, economic, and political issues.

However, government actions and legislation have often undermined the ability of such groups to function. Despite a limited flowering of civil society since 2001, civic, political, and labor organizations have functioned with difficulty, with authorities harassing, arresting, and prosecuting their leaders and members. This has intensified in the wake of widespread pro-democracy demonstrations throughout much of the country in February and March 2011. In particular, the Ministry of Social Development has far exceeded international standards in its restrictive scope and "routinely exploited its oversight role to stymie the activities of NGOs and other civil society organizations."[1]

Today, freedom of association is under even greater threat due in part to draft legislation that is even more restrictive than the current Law of Associations (No. 21/1989), which authorities use—in the words of one Bahraini activist—"to interfere, restrict, and attempt to control the activities of civic organizations."

This report examines restrictions on civil societies, political groups, and trade unions in Bahrain through three main lenses: current laws, the draft laws (where relevant), and applicable international standards, using case studies as illustration where possible.

---

[1] US State Department, Bureau of Democracy, Human Rights, and Labor, "Country Reports on Human Rights Practices – 2010: Bahrain," April 11, 2011, http://www.state.gov/j/drl/rls/hrrpt/2010/nea/154459.htm (accessed October 9, 2012).

Current Laws

The present Law of Associations prohibits civil society organizations from "engaging in politics" and lets authorities dissolve organizations more or less at will. Amended in 2002, it also prohibits activities that could affect "the foundations of the Islamic faith or the unity of the people or stirs a discord or sectarianism."

The report finds that authorities use the law to suppress civil society and restrict freedom of association in three main ways: by arbitrarily rejecting registration applications and intrusively supervising NGOs; taking over and dissolving—more or less at will—organizations whose leaders have criticized government officials or their policies; and severely limiting the ability of groups to fundraise and receive foreign funding. For example:

- In September 2004, authorities dissolved the Bahrain Center for Human Rights after its president criticized the prime minister;
- In September 2010, the Ministry of Social Development replaced the Bahrain Human Rights Society's board after its secretary general criticized authorities for violating the due process rights of detained opposition activists;
- In April 2011, the Ministry of Social Development dissolved the Bahrain Teachers' Society after its leaders took part in February-March 2011 pro-democracy protests;
- In April 2011, authorities replaced Bahrain Medical Society's board members with a pro-government board;
- In November 2011, the ministry canceled the results of Bahrain Lawyers' Society election after the group elected perceived government critics to the board.

In the case of political societies, the report shows how authorities have used the current Law for Political Societies (Law No. 26/2005), the Public Gathering Law of 1973, and the Press Law of 2002 to prohibit political parties and control their freedom of association, expression, and peaceful assembly. Authorities do not have to give a reason when they deny registration to a political society, which can be suspended if it "violates" legal or constitutional provisions. Political groups cannot contact political groups outside Bahrain without official approval and may not accept "donations" or "benefit" from a foreign person or entity. Recent restrictive measures highlighted in this report include:

- In May 2005, authorities shuttered the offices of the Islamic Action Society (Amal) for 45 days after it held an event to honor 73 individuals jailed for allegedly planning a coup in 1981;
- In March and April 2011, security forces arrested dozens of protest leaders, including Ibrahim Sharif, leader of the leftist National Democratic Action Society (Wa'ad) and Shaikh Muhammad Ali al-Mahfoodh of the Islamic Action Society (Amal).
- In April 2011, the Bahrain Defense Force shut down Wa'ad and blocked its website for more than two months on charges of "defaming the armed forces and spreading false news."
- In June 2011, a special military court convicted Sharif and 20 other protest leaders—seven in absentia—and sentenced them to prison terms of up to life imprisonment for offenses relating to the exercise of freedom of expression, assembly, and association.
- In July 2012, a court dissolved the Amal political society for failing to "convene a general conference for more than four years" and "taking its decisions from a religious authority who calls openly for violence and incites hatred."

Under Bahrain's Workers Trade Union Law (33/2002), workers can establish trade unions without prior official approval, although authorities do not let public sector workers create unions. This report shows how the law and other government regulations impose numerous restrictions on the right to strike and prohibit strikes in "vital and important facilities" such as "security, civil defense, airports, ports, hospitals, transportations, telecommunications, electricity and water facilities" and near "bakeries, all means of transporting people and goods, educational establishments and oil and gas installations."

In 2011, King Hamad bin Isa Al Khalifa amended the Trade Union Law to allow more than one trade union federation in Bahrain, a move many unionists consider to be retribution for the call by the General Federation of Bahrain Trade Unions (GFBTU) for mass labor strikes during the February-March pro-democracy demonstrations in 2011. After the amendment came into force in March 2012, government loyalists established the Bahrain Free Labour Unions Federation (BFLUF). The new federation has accused the GFBTU of being a political tool of the opposition groups. The king's amendment also granted the minister of labor the power to decide which trade union confederation will engage in collective bargaining at the national level and represent Bahrain in international meetings and events.

Draft Law of Associations

In February 2013, Human Rights Watch obtained a copy of the 2012 Draft Law on Civil Organizations and Institutions (Draft Law of Associations) that the government adopted in August 2012. It needs approval from both National Assembly houses—the elected Chamber of Deputies and appointed Shura Council—and King Hamad's signature to become law. It was not clear at time of writing when the house would approve the law, or when the king would sign it into law.

The draft law, which the government sent to parliament in January 2013 without consulting or informing local organizations, follows years of failing to pass draft legislation that would liberalize the process of forming and running civil society organizations.

Several of its provisions are even more draconian than the current 1989 law. They include increasing the required number of founding members from 10 to 15. The current law does not require applicants to provide operation budgets, but the draft law requires an organization seeking to register to have a "two year operational budget" and to provide evidence that it has a physical office. Similarly the current law does not prohibit applicants from seeking to register a dissolved NGO. The draft law prohibits any effort "to revive another NGO that was dissolved or merged into another organization."

International and Bahraini Law

The International Covenant on Civil and Political Rights (ICCPR), to which Bahrain is party, clearly establishes the rights to freedom of association and participation in public affairs.

The ICCPR does allow for some narrow restrictions on the right to freedom of association that are necessary for the protection of "national security or public safety, public order (*ordre public*), the protection of public health or morals" and these restrictions are subjected to a rigorous test. For example the term "national security" and "public safety" refer to a situation involving immediate and violent threat to the entire nation.

Bahraini laws and regulations do not adequately guarantee the right to freedom of association as set out in in the ICCPR. Bahraini authorities have decreed and drafted laws that significantly narrow the opportunities for establishing and operating political and civic associations and trade unions, and unduly restrict their capacity to function.

Necessary Steps

Human Rights Watch calls on the Bahraini government to amend existing laws and draft legislation that allow the government to control and suppress the legitimate activities of NGOs, labor unions, and political groups and to prosecute their leaders and members for exercising their right to freedom of association. These include:

- Releasing all leaders and activists with opposition NGOs and political societies who have been jailed solely for the exercise of the rights to freedom of expression, association, and peaceful assembly, and expunging their convictions.
- Amending the 2012 Draft Law of Associations to bring it into conformity with the International Covenant on Civil and Political Rights (ICCPR) by lifting broad restrictions and prohibitions on the right to freedom of association except for legitimate reasons defined under article 22 (2) of the ICCPR.
- Amending article 4 (4) of the Political Societies Law (No. 26/2005) to abolish the overly broad provision that prohibits establishing political societies on the basis of "class, sect, geography, profession, religion, language, race or sex."
- Respecting and promoting the rights of workers by amending the Workers Trade Union Law (Law 33/2002) to allow public sector workers to create and join trade unions in accordance with Bahrain's obligations under the ICCPR.

Human Rights Watch also urges the government to consult with civil society, including opposition groups and political societies, when amending current association-related laws and proposing new legislation. Only by ceasing unjustifiable interference with the exercise of the right to freedom of association can the government meet its obligations under international human rights law.

Key Recommendations

To the Government of Bahrain

In order to comply with international obligations regarding freedom of association:

- Remove all unjustifiable restrictions on the peaceful exercise of the internationally recognized rights to freedom of association and freedom to participate in public life;
- Release all leaders and activists with opposition NGOs and political societies who have been jailed solely for the exercise of the rights to freedom of expression, association, and peaceful assembly, and expunging their convictions;
- Amend article 2 of the Draft Law on Civil Organizations and Institutions to eliminate restrictions on establishing NGOs on "a factional or sectarian basis or to achieve objectives contrary to the provisions of the constitution or legislation in force in the Kingdom of Bahrain, or the public order and morals, or [if their] activities include engaging in politics";
- Amend article 8 of the Draft Law on Civil Organizations and Institutions to specify that the absence of a Ministry of Social Development response to a registration request by a civic organization within 60 days means that approval has been given;
- Amend article 4 (4) of the Political Societies Law (No. 26/2005) to eliminate restrictions on establishing political society on the basis of "class, sect, geography, profession, religion, language, race or sex";
- Amend the Workers Trade Union Law (Law 33/2002) to allow public sector workers to create and join trade unions; and
- Ratify key International Labour Organization conventions, such as the Freedom of Association and Protection of the Right to Organise Convention, 1948 (No. 87) and the Right to Organise and Collective Bargaining Convention, 1949 (No. 98).

Methodology

Human Rights Watch researchers visited Bahrain for two weeks in November-December 2011 and again briefly in February 2013, and met with more than two dozen members of civic associations, trade unions, and political societies.

During this period Bahrain did not respond to multiple visa requests by the Human Rights Watch researcher responsible for this report to visit Bahrain.

Human Rights Watch conducted additional interviews, most of them in Arabic, via telephone and Skype with approximately 30 other NGO, trade union, and political society leaders and members. All interview subjects consented to take part in our interviews and were informed that the interviews were to be in a human rights report. In some cases the report withholds the identities of sources to protect their safety and privacy. Human Rights watch did not offer interview subjects any remuneration.

Representatives of the NGOs, workers' unions and political societies provided Human Rights Watch with copies of official documents, without remuneration, pertaining to the cases discussed in this report. Human Rights Watch also obtained documents available on websites affiliated with the Bahraini government. All of these documents are on file with Human Rights Watch.

Human Rights Watch learned about case studies mentioned in this report from media reports and from members of NGOs, workers' unions, and political societies. There may be cases that Human Rights Watch is not aware of, and thus has not included here.

The report also draws on accounts, from 1998 to 2013, relating to the cases covered in this report published by pro-government and independent media in Bahrain as well as international media.

In February 2013, a delegation of Human Rights Watch met with the Ministry of Social Development's officials and discussed some of the issues raised in this report. On May 13, 2013, Human Rights Watch sent a letter to the Ministry of Social Development summarizing its findings and conclusions, and asking for comments and clarifications, to which the ministry did not respond.

I. Background

Civil Society in Bahrain

Around half of Bahrain's population of 1.2 million are Bahraini nationals; the rest are migrant and expatriate workers. Some 60 percent of Bahraini nationals are Shia Muslims.[2] The ruling Al Khalifa family, who are Sunni Muslims, control all key political government posts, security positions, and important economic institutions.

During the 20th century, civic, political, and trade union organizations played increasingly important roles in shaping Bahrain, a British protectorate between 1868 and 1971. Since 1995, Bahrain has been home to the US Navy's Fifth Fleet.

In 1938, for example, workers at the Bahrain Petroleum Company (Bapco) organized a strike to protest the company's prioritizing foreign workers over Bahrainis when hiring. Bahrainis advocating for labor rights and a representative government established the Higher Executive Committee (later the National Union Committee) in 1954. After protests erupted in 1956, British authorities deported several of the group's leaders to the South Atlantic island of St. Helena, where they spent five years in exile.

The early 1990s witnessed public demonstrations and petitions calling for greater civil and political rights in Bahrain and restoration of the National Assembly. The ruling family stood firmly against reforms, leading to widespread arrests of peaceful protesters as well as those who clashed with security forces.[3]

After becoming emir in 1999, Hamad bin Isa Al Khalifa oversaw a number of significant political reforms, including cancelling in February 2001 the State Security Law, abolishing state security courts, pardoning hundreds of political prisoners, and issuing amnesties for exiled political figures.[4]

---

2 "Bahrain: People and Society", Central Intelligence Agency, The World Factbook 2013, updated May 7, 2013, https://www.cia.gov/library/publications/the-world-factbook/geos/ba.html (accessed June 3, 2013).

Human Rights Watch, *Routine Abuse, Routine Denial*, July 1, 1997, http://www.hrw.org/legacy/reports/1997/bahrain/.

3 See: Human Rights Watch news release, "Bahrain Prisoner Release, Open Debate Welcome," February 12, 2001, http://www.hrw.org/news/2001/02/11/bahrain-prisoner-release-open-debate-welcome. . Shaikh Hamad changed his title to king in 2002.

Since 2001, scores of civic, labor, and political organizations have emerged in Bahrain. However, the authorities have continued to harass and prosecute leaders and members of civic and political organizations critical of government policies, a campaign that has escalated in the wake of the February-March 2011 political crisis.

On February 14, 2011, thousands of Bahrainis came out in street demonstrations in several parts of the country demanding greater political rights and government reform. Security forces used lethal force to suppress and disperse demonstrators.

Government repression of the civic, labor, and political organizations intensified after King Hamad declared a three-month state of emergency in mid-March 2011. Security forces launched a campaign of retribution and arrested thousands who participated in, or appeared to support, the largely peaceful protests, including leaders of opposition political groups, civic organizations, and labor unions. Civilian and special military courts sentenced hundreds of people accused of involvement with the protests in unfair trials.

Since the 2011 crackdown, authorities have amended a number of laws that would make it even harder for civic organizations to operate. This report examines the relevant laws and draft laws that authorities have used or proposed to further restrict freedom of association in Bahrain.

II. Civil Society Organizations

> Civil society organizations have to report every idea, thought, and activity to authorities…. All these hinder the abilities of the societies. There is a huge attack on civil associations in Bahrain.
> —Rula al-Saffar, president of the Bahrain Nursing Society, August 8, 2012.[5]

Civic engagement and political activism in Bahrain predate independence from British rule in 1971. For the past several decades, social, cultural, and sports clubs, as well as civil and professional organizations, have played important roles in shaping political debate in the country. Given the prohibition on political groups until 2001, NGOs often served as forums for discussing social, economic, and political issues.[6]

In 1989, the government issued by decree the Law of Associations, Social and Cultural Clubs, Special Committees Working in the Field of Youth and Sports, and Private Institutions (Law of Associations No. 21/1989). The law, among other things, prohibits civil society organizations from "engaging in politics."[7] In 2002, King Hamad bin Isa Al Khalifa amended the law to also prohibit activities that could affect "the foundations of the Islamic faith or the unity of the people or stirs discord or sectarianism."[8]

The authorities use the law, in the words of one Bahraini activist, "to interfere, restrict, and attempt to control the activities of civic organizations."[9]

Authorities have used this law to clamp down on organizations arbitrarily, especially targeting those involved in peaceful dissent, or which have supported political opposition groups. In 2011, authorities invoked the Law of Associations to dissolve, take over, or suspend organizations that supported pro-democracy demonstrations that swept the

---

[5] Human Rights Watch, phone conversation with Rula al-Saffar, president of Bahrain Nursing Society, August 8, 2012.

[6] Emile Nakhleh, *Bahrain: Political Development in a Modernizing Society* (Maryland: Lexington Books, 2011), p.41.

[7] Law No 21/1989, art. 18. Translation provided by the International Center for Not-for-Profit Law.

[8] "Decree No. 44 of year 2002 to amend some provisions of the Law of Associations…., (مرسوم بقانون رقم (44) لسنة 2002 بتعديل بعض أحكام قانون الجمعيات)," Legislation and Legal Opinion Commission, http://www.legalaffairs.gov.bh/viewhtm.aspx?ID=L4402 (accessed December 6, 2012).

[9] Human Rights Watch, email correspondence with Ala'a Shehabi, Bahrain Rehabilitation and Anti-Violence Organization (BRAVO), May 15, 2012.

country in February and March that year. In April 2011, the Ministry of Social Development dissolved the Bahrain Teachers' Society and replaced the board of the Bahrain Medical Society. Both organizations had supported demonstrators' demands for greater political rights.

Authorities freely used the provisions of the law against civil society organizations in earlier periods as well. In January 1998, for example, the government reacted swiftly when the Bahrain Lawyers' Society (BLS) held a seminar in which speakers criticized the government.[10] The Ministry of Labor and Social Development, then in charge of civil groups, suspended its board of directors because it had allegedly "engaged in political activities."[11] The society successfully appealed the decision at an administrative court.

In September 2004, the government dissolved the Bahrain Center for Human Rights after its then-president, Abd al-Hadi al-Khawaja, criticized the prime minister for his economic policies, alleged corruption, and human rights abuses.[12] A court convicted al-Khawaja of "inciting hatred against the regime."[13]

In August 2007, the Ministry of Social Development threatened legal action against the Bahrain Women's Association after the organization invited women rights activists to Bahrain without getting prior permission from the ministry.[14]

In August 2010, the ministry threatened to shut down a women's shelter managed by the Bahrain Migrant Workers Protection Society (MWPS) following an incident in which a migrant domestic worker fled to the shelter from the home of a high ministry official, claiming she had been abused. The ministry claimed that the society had not registered the shelter. The head of MWPS responded with a copy of the government's 2005

---

[10] "Bar Association Confiscated in Bahrain, (مصادرة جمعية المحامين البحرينية)," Arab Commission for Human Rights, November 1998, http://www.achr.nu/rep14.htm (accessed August 1, 2012).

[11] Ibid.

[12] The BCHR still operates in Bahrain although its leaders are increasingly subjected to harassment and arrest.

[13] Al-Khawaja received a one-year prison sentence but King Hamad bin Isa al Khalifa pardoned him on November 21, 2004 just hours after the court convicted him. See "Bahrain: Rights Center Closed as Crackdown Expands," Human Rights Watch, news release, September 30, 2004, http://www.hrw.org/news/2004/09/29/bahrain-rights-center-closed-crackdown-expands.

[14] "The Ministry of Social Development takes legal procedures against Women's Association, (التنمية تبدأ اتخاذ الإجراءات القانونية ضد البحرين النسائية)," Akhbar al-Khaleej, August 26, 2007, http://www.akhbar-alkhaleej.com/10747/article/199706.html (accessed October 19, 2012).

authorization of the shelter, and noted that in previous years the ministry itself had donated funds to support the shelter.[15]

This chapter examines three main areas regarding restrictions on freedom of association and suppression of civil society in Bahrain:

- Arbitrary rejection of registration applications and intrusive governmental supervision of NGOs;
- Takeover and in some cases dissolution of organizations whose leaders have criticized government officials or their policies;
- Considerable limits placed on the ability of groups to fund raise and receive foreign funding.

In each of these three areas the report examines current applicable law, the provisions of the draft law under consideration that relate to the issue, and applicable international standards. Case studies illustrate how authorities have used the law to harass and, in some cases, outlaw civic groups that have been critical of the government or its policies.

Freedom of Association/Civil Society Repression

International

The right to freedom of association is well established under the International Covenant on Civil and Political Rights (ICCPR), to which Bahrain is party. Article 22 of the ICCPR states: "Everyone shall have the right to freedom of association with others."[16] As such, it is "not something that must first be granted by the government to citizens."[17] The ICCPR does allow for some narrow restrictions on the right to freedom of association but subjects these to a rigorous test, as defined by the ICCPR in article 22 (2).

---

[15] Human Rights Watch, World Report 2011 (New York: Human Rights Watch, 2011), Bahrain chapter, http://www.hrw.org/world-report-2011/world-report-2011-bahrain.

[16] International Covenant on Civil and Political Rights (ICCPR), adopted December 16, 1966, G.A. Res. 2200A (XXI), 21 UN GAOR Supp. (No. 16) at 52, UN Doc. A/6316 (1966), 999 UNT.S. 171, entered into force March 23, 1976. Bahrain ratified the ICCPR in 2006.

[17] Public Interest Law Initiative, *Enabling Civil Society: Practical Aspects of Freedom of Association Source Book* (Budapest, Public Interest Law Initiative, Columbia University Budapest Law Center, 2003).

No restrictions may be placed on the exercise of this right other than those
which are prescribed by law and which are necessary in a democratic
society in the interests of national security or public safety, public order
(*ordre public*), the protection of public health or morals or the protection of
the rights and freedoms of others.

The term "national security" refers to "a political or military threat to the entire nation or that disseminates propaganda for war." "Public safety" refers to threats to "the security of persons (i.e., their lives, physical integrity or health)."[18]

Professor Manfred Nowak, in his authoritative commentary on the ICCPR, wrote that while article 22 protects associations, states may require a licensing system, including a registration duty.[19] Any restriction done for a legitimate reason must still be "proportional and be oriented along the basic democratic values of pluralism, tolerance, broad-mindedness and peoples' sovereignty."[20]

Bahrain has also ratified the Arab League's Arab Charter for Human Rights, which affirms that citizens have the right to "freely form and join associations with others."[21]

Bahraini Law

Article 27 of Bahrain's 2002 Constitution guarantees the freedom to establish associations and unions "under the rules and conditions laid down by law," provided their objectives are lawful and carried out by peaceful means and do not infringe on "the fundamentals of religion and public order."[22]

---

[18] Manfred Nowak, *UN Covenant on Civil and Political Rights. CCPR Commentary* (Kehl Am Rhein, Germany: N.P. Engel, 2005), p. 506.

[19] Ibid. The International Center for Not-for-Profit Law (ICNL), which provides information on the legal issues for civic organizations, says that that the ICCPR does not require individuals to " form legal entities in order to exercise their freedoms of expression, and association." Leon E. Irish, Robert Kushen, and Karla W. Simon, *Guidelines for Laws Affecting Civic Organizations* (New York: Open Society Institute, 2004), p. 21.

[20] Manfred Nowak, *U.N. Covenant on Civil and Political Rights: CCPR Commentary* (Kehl: N.P. Engel, 1993), p. 394.

[21] Art. 24 (5,6,7) says, "No restrictions may be placed on the exercise of these rights other than those which are prescribed by law and which are necessary in a democratic society in the interests of national security or public safety, public health or morals or the protection of the rights and freedoms of others."
http://www1.umn.edu/humanrts/instree/loas2005.html?msource=UNWDEC19001&tr=y&auid=3337655 (accessed April 4 2012).

[22] Bahrain Constitution, art. 27.

In practice, Bahraini authorities have used loosely worded provisions of the current Law of Associations and other laws to significantly narrow the scope for establishing and operating political and civic associations and restrict their capacity to function. For example, article 18 of the 1989 Law of Associations says that organizations "may not get involved in politics" and article 50 says that authorities can dissolve NGOs if they think the NGOs are "unable to achieve the objectives [they were] established for… or if they violate the association law, public order and norms." Thus the law provides numerous ways for authorities to interfere arbitrarily with NGO affairs and shut them down.

The law requires that all civil society groups, even informal ones, register with authorities. Article 89 of the 1989 law stipulates a fine of 500 Bahraini Dinars (US$1,320) and/or six months' imprisonment for establishing and operating an unregistered organization.[23] Article 163 of Bahrain's penal code also criminalizes membership in unlicensed organizations in Bahrain or in organizations outside of the country.[24] In November 2010, King Hamad bin Isa Al Khalifa signed an amendment to article 89 of the 1989 law specifying penalties of up to one year in prison and/or a fine of up to 1,000 Bahraini Dinars ($2,640) for anyone who publishes or broadcasts anything on behalf of an organization operating without a license.[25]

In 2007, the Ministry of Social Development, which since 2005 has been in charge of implementing the Law of Associations and overseeing civil society groups' affairs, announced plans to replace the 1989 Law of Associations.[26] In April 2007, Minister of Social Development Fatima al-Balooshi said the legislation "will be passed within months."[27] *Al-Wasat*, Bahrain's only independent daily, published the draft law in

---

[23] Law No 21/1989, art. 89(2), Translation provided by the International Center for Not-for-Profit Law. Article 87 (1) stipulates a fine of 1,000 Bahraini Dinars ($2,640) and/or imprisonment for establishing and operating an unregistered organization. Draft Law on Civil Organizations and Institutions, art. 87 (1)

[24] Law No 1 5/1976, Penal Code, art. 163: Any person who joins the aforesaid societies, organizations, and institutions, shall be liable for imprisonment for a period of no more than 3 months or a fine not exceeding 30 Dinars. The same penalty shall apply to any citizen residing in the State of Bahrain for joining or participating in any manner without a Government license in any of the aforesaid organizations, which are based outside the country.

[25] "Decree No. 50/2010, (مرسوم بقانون رقم (50) لسنة 2012)," *Official Gazette*, November 25, 2010, http://www.legalaffairs.gov.bh/viewpdf.aspx?ID=L5010 (accessed July 15, 2012).

[26] Until January 2005 the Ministry of Labor and Social Affairs managed NGOs' affairs. Since January 2005 the Ministry of Social Development has been managing civic organizations.

[27] "Al-Balooshi: New law for associations within months, (البلوشي: قانون الجمعيات الجديد خلال أشهر)," *Al-Waqt*, April 5, 2007, http://www.alwaqt.com/art.php?aid=48914 (accessed May 24, 2012).

September 2009.[28] Authorities after 2007 did not provide updates on the status of the draft until August 2011, at which time al-Balooshi said the government was "preparing a final version of the new draft law for private organizations after inserting draft amendments."[29]

In May 2012, Human Rights Watch wrote to the ministry requesting a copy of the draft law, and sent further requests for a copy of the law after it was reportedly submitted to the Chamber of Deputies. The ministry did not respond.[30]

On August 12, 2012, the Bahrain News Agency reported that the Council of Ministers had adopted a draft Law of Associations.[31] The process had no transparency whatsoever. Local organizations told Human Rights Watch that authorities did not consult them ahead of passing the legislation and that they were not aware of its adoption until media reported it.[32] On August 15, 2012, Najwa Janahi, director of NGO affairs in the ministry, claimed that the government had consulted representatives of civic organizations and experts in 2007, although the 2012 draft bore little resemblance to the draft of 2007 and is in some respects more restrictive than the current 1989 law.[33]

---

[28] The newspaper published the draft law in three issues starting on September 7, 2009: "Al-Wasat publishes the new draft law of associations, (الوسط تنشر مسودة قانون المنظمات الجديد)," *Al-Wasat*, September 7, 2009, http://www.alwasatnews.com/2558/news/read/309598/1.html, *Al-Wasat*, September 8, 2009, http://www.alwasatnews.com/2559/news/read/309751/1.html, *Al-Wasat*, September 8, 2009, http://www.alwasatnews.com/2560/news/read/309887/1.html, *Al-Wasat*, September 9, 2009, (accessed December 6, 2012).

[29] "Al-Balooshi: Banning the mix of political and human rights work … and setting regulations for associations' external relations, (البلوشي: منع الجمع بين العملين السياسي والحقوقي... وضوابط لعلاقة الجمعيات بالخارج)," *Al-Wasat*, August 18, 2011, http://www.alwasatnews.com/3267/news/read/583979/1.html (accessed April 3, 2012). In July 2011, the government sponsored what it called a National Dialogue which it said aimed at presenting "the people's views and demands for further reform." The vast majority of the 350 participants were government supporters. With regard to civic organizations the participants proposed a "National Strategy for NGOs" which specified that organizations should "should not combine political and human rights activities." See "National Dialogue; Outcomes," The National Dialogue http://www.nd.bh/en/index.php/the-dialogue/executive-summary-of-outcomes#social, (accessed March 16, 2013).

[30] Human Rights Watch wrote to the ministry requesting a copy of the draft law on May 14, 2012. Human Rights Watch sent follow-up emails to the ministry on May 30, June 13, August 7, August 14, August 29, September 4, September 10, October 9 October 29, 2012.

[31] "Dr. al-Balooshi: New private associations law contains huge rights and achievements, (الدكتورة البلوشي: قانون المنظمات الأهلية الجديد يتضمن حقوقا ومكاسب كبيرة)," *Bahrain News Agency*, August 13, 2012, http://bna.bh/portal/news/520718 (accessed August 14, 2012).

[32] "CSOs express concerns on restrictions of Law of Associations, (جمعيات تُبدي تخوفاً من تقييد قانون المنظمات للعمل الأهلي)," *Al-Wasat*, August 14, 2012, http://www.alwasatnews.com/3629/news/read/694371/1.html (accessed August 14, 2012).

[33] "Janahi: the Ministry of Social Development discussed the [draft] Law on Associations with NGOs in workshops and meetings, (جناحي: «التنمية» ناقشت «قانون المنظمات» مع الجمعيات خلال ورش العمل واللقاءات)," *Al-Wasat*, August 15, 2012, http://www.alwasatnews.com/3630/news/read/694587/1.html, (accessed March 16, 2013).

During its visit to Bahrain in February 2013, Human Rights Watch obtained a copy of the draft law adopted by the government and submitted to the Chamber of Deputies.[34]

The following analysis of the most problematic restrictions on NGOs is based on the Draft Law of Associations that Human Rights Watch obtained in February 2013.

Registering and Supervising NGOs

Current Law

Law 21/1989 authorizes Bahraini authorities to control civil society groups via the registration process and strictly supervise their activities. All organizations must register with authorities prior to undertaking activities.

The Ministry of Social Development is responsible for registering all organizations except "cultural and artistic associations," which the Ministry of Information supervises.[35] Under the current law, the General Organization for Youth and Sports is responsible for registering and managing "youth and sports ... clubs."[36]

The government provides funds for NGO activities that the Ministry of Social Development approves.[37] Once they do register, NGOs are subject to intense official scrutiny and, if critical of government officials and policies, are targets of official harassment. The ministry can rescind an NGO's status at any time.

---

34 The "Draft Law on Civil Organizations and Institutions," on file with Human Rights Watch, was signed by Prime Minister Khalifa bin Salman Al Khalifa and sent to the Chamber of Deputies on January 14, 2013. Human Rights Watch requested a copy at a meeting with ministry officials on February 27, 2013, but the officials would not provide it. Human Rights Watch subsequently received a copy from a Bahraini civil society activist.

35 According to documents published by the *Official Gazette* between 1991 and 2003 the Ministry of Information registered 18 cultural and artistic associations; The First Theater, Jazeera Theater, Bahrain Archeology and History Association, Bahraini Family of Intellectuals and Writers' Association, Bahrain Fine Arts Association, Bahrain Contemporary Arts Association, the Media Association of the Gulf Cooperation States, Bahrain Music and Popular Arts Association, Bahrain Club for Cinema, Bahrain Pottery Association, Al-Sawari Theater, Bahrain Bookstores Association, the Popular Heritage Association, Bahrain Gratification Association, the Popular Poems Association, Bahrain Journalists Association, the Private Cultural Forum Association, and the Bahrain Internet Association.

36 Law No 21/1989, preamble.

37 Human Rights Watch meeting with Khalid al-Koheji, assistant under-secretary for community affairs, who is responsible for nongovernmental groups, Sultan Hammadi, the ministry's legal counselor for nongovernmental group affairs, Manama, February 27, 2013.

The authorities take advantage of the fact that Law 21/1989 contains broadly worded provisions that allow them to deny an organization's request to register if, for example, authorities determine that "society does not need its services or if there are other associations that fulfill the society's need."[38]

To start the registration process, the applicant has to submit information about the organization's founders (at least 10 persons under the 1989 law); its purpose and geographic area of activities; its sources of income and internal auditing procedures; conditions for accepting and dismissing members; and its mechanism to elect board members and dissolve the organization.[39]

The application is considered rejected if the ministry does not respond within 60 days.[40]

The applicant can appeal a registration denial to the minister of social development and subsequently to the High Civil Court. The court reviews officials' compliance with the formalities of registration under the Law of Association and tests whether the officials properly used their authority to deny a registration.[41]

The 1989 law also grants government officials the power to monitor and intervene in the activities and management of recognized NGOs. For example, the Ministry of Social Development can decide to merge organizations that it concludes work to "achieve similar aims."[42] Civil society organizations must notify authorities 15 days before holding general assembly meetings, which authorities can attend.[43] They must also inform authorities of any decision that the board takes within 15 days of the meeting.[44]

The ministry can also overturn NGO decisions if authorities consider that they violate the NGO's bylaws "or public order and norms."[45] The law requires NGOs to get permission to organize any fundraising events, and specifies that a group submit bank account

---

[38] Law No 21/1989, art. 11.

[39] Ibid., art. 5 (1-8).

[40] Law No 21/1989, art. 11.

[41] Ibid., art. 12 (2).

[42] Ibid., art.24.

[43] Ibid., art. 33.

[44] Ibid., arts. 45, 46.

[45] Ibid., art. 28.

information to authorities, who can freeze a group's funds and accounts.[46] Authorities can request that an organization provide any and all records, documents, and correspondence.[47]

Draft Law

The August 2012 Draft Law of Associations (Draft Law on Civil Organizations and Institutions) that the government submitted to the National Assembly in January 2013 removed most of the improved features of the 2007 draft law and maintained many highly restrictive features of the existing law regarding NGO registration and ministry control over the affairs of civil society organizations. Some provisions of the new law are even more burdensome than the current law.

For example, article 2 of the draft law would add a new provision that would prohibit establishing NGOs on "a factional or sectarian basis or to achieve objectives contrary to the provisions of the constitution or legislation in force in the Kingdom of Bahrain, or the public order and morals, or [if their] activities include engaging in politics."[48]

Professor Manfred Nowak, in his commentary on the ICCPR, wrote that "the principles of equality and the prohibition of discrimination runs like a red thread throughout the [ICCPR]." Article 26 of the ICCPR, he wrote, guarantees "equal protection of the law, as well as a general prohibition of discrimination,"[49] adding that "the freedom to proclaim political beliefs is principally ensured by the political freedoms in [articles] 19, 20, 21 [and 25 of the ICCPR]."

The language of article 2 of the 2012 draft law is overly broad and the words 'factional or sectarian basis' would appear to allow the discriminatory prohibition of NGOs specifically on their political or religious beliefs.

---

[46] Ibid., arts. 21 and 17.

[47] Ibid., art. 15.

[48] Draft Law on Civil Organizations and Institutions, art. 2.

[49] Article 26 of the ICCPR says: "All persons are equal before the law and are entitled without any discrimination to the equal protection of the law. In this respect, the law shall prohibit any discrimination and guarantee to all persons equal and effective protection against discrimination on any ground such as race, colour, sex, language, religion, political or other opinion, national or social origin, property, birth or other status." See: Manfred Nowak, *UN Covenant on Civil and Political Rights. CCPR Commentary* (Kehl Am Rhein, Germany: N.P. Engel, 2005), p. 597, 600.

The Ministry of Social Development can reject the registration of an NGO if it determines that "[Bahraini] society does not need its services … or if [the NGO was founded] in order to revive another NGO that was dissolved or merged into another organization."[50]

The 2012 draft law increases the required number of founding members from 10 to 15.[51] The draft legislation requires that an organization seeking to register has a "two year operational budget" and to provide evidence that it has a physical office.[52]

As in the present law, an organization's application is considered rejected if the ministry does not expressly approve it within 60 days.[53] The applicant can appeal a denial to a ministerial committee, appointed by the minister, which should review the appeal within 60 days of receiving it.[54] The appeal is considered denied if the committee does not respond within 60 days.[55] The applicant can then appeal the ministerial committee's denial to the administrative court within 60 days of learning about the denial.[56]

The draft law also prohibits a member of one NGO from joining another NGO if the two organizations "conduct similar activities, unless approved by the minister."[57]

Nongovernmental organizations must notify authorities 15 days before holding general assembly meetings, which authorities can attend.[58] Organizations must also inform authorities of any decision that the board takes within 10 days of the meeting, as opposed to 15 days under the current law.[59]

Under the draft law the ministry retains authority to merge NGOs "if they work to achieve similar objectives … or to modify their purposes depending on the needs of the society… or for other reasons."[60] The ministry's approval is needed if an organization wants to affiliate

---

[50] Draft Law on Civil Organizations and Institutions, art. 8.

[51] Ibid., art. 3.

[52] Ibid., art. 6 (4), (5).

[53] Ibid., art. 8.

[54] Ibid., art. 9.

[55] Ibid., art. 9.

[56] Ibid. The draft law does not indicate any time period in which the administrative court should respond.

[57] Ibid., art. 7.

[58] Ibid., art. 27.

[59] Ibid., art. 40.

[60] Ibid., art. 22.

or collaborate with an organization outside Bahrain; in this case approval is automatic if the ministry does not object within 90 days of receiving notification.[61]

Under article 88 of the draft law NGOs also need prior permission from "the minister [of social development] and relevant authorities" to invite foreigners to visit Bahrain for activities such as conferences and forums.[62] Article 87 (9) stipulates a fine of 1,000 Bahraini Dinars (US$2,640) and/or imprisonment for violating article 88.[63]

Recommended Standards

The *Guidelines for Laws Affecting Civic Organizations*, a handbook published by the Open Society Institute in cooperation with the International Center for Not-for-Profit Law (ICNL), recommends that laws governing the right of association "should be written and administered so that it is quick, easy, and inexpensive to establish a civic organization as a legal person."[64]

Laws regarding establishment of NGOs should set short time frames for authorities to review an application "e.g., a maximum of 60 days," and failure to do so "should result in presumptive approval."[65] Aspiring NGOs should not be required to prove that they are able to accomplish stated objectives.[66] The ICNL also recommends that NGOs should be permitted to "embrace all activities" that "would be legal if engaged in by any individual," including politics.[67]

In any case in which the state authority rejects an application, the ICNL says, "the responsible state agency should be required to provide a detailed written statement of reasons for refusal" and "an opportunity to correct any defects in the application," and the refusal should be "appealable to an independent court."[68]

---

[61] Ibid., art. 16.

[62] Ibid., art. 88.

[63] Ibid., art. 87 (9).

[64] Leon E. Irish, Robert Kushen, and Karla W. Simon, *Guidelines for Laws Affecting Civic Organizations* (New York: Open Society Institute, 2004), p. 26.

[65] Leon E. Irish, Robert Kushen, and Karla W. Simon, *Guidelines for Laws Affecting Civic Organizations* (New York: Open Society Institute, 2004), p 27.

[66] Ibid., p. 28.

[67] Ibid., p. 28.

[68] Ibid., p. 27, 28.

The ICNL recommends that only organizations that have "significant public benefit activities or [operate] with substantial public support" be required to file annual financial and activities reports with a regulatory body, provided that the latter "protect(s) the legitimate privacy interests of donors and recipients of benefits as well as the protection of confidential or proprietary information."[69]

While the ICNL acknowledges that it may be reasonable for a regulatory body to examine records and activities of organizations "during ordinary business hours, with adequate advance notice," it argues that those powers should not be used to "inhibit the freedom of association of the individuals" or harass the organization.[70]

The ICNL recommends that authorities set "clear rules" to allow "but not compel" NGOs to merge, split, or modify themselves. However, it states that authorities could set conditions on the ability of NGOs to merge with "for-profit entities."[71]

The Ministry of Social Development's restrictive approach to Bahraini NGOs goes well beyond what international standards stipulate, as the following case studies illustrate. As one US State Department report noted, Bahraini civil society activists have complained that the ministry has "routinely exploited its oversight role to stymie the activities of NGOs and other civil society organizations."[72]

Case Studies

The 1989 Law of Associations now in force does not require authorities to notify aspiring NGOs when they reject an application to register. Human Rights Watch is aware of several cases—some of which are detailed below—of authorities refusing to register would-be NGOs that media have reported or that Bahraini activists brought to Human Rights Watch's attention.[73]

---

[69] Ibid., p. 26.

[70] "Checklist for NGO Laws," International Center for Not-for-Profit Law. 2006, http://www.humanitarianforum.org/data/files/resources/704/en/ICNL-NPOChecklist.pdf, p. 7.

[71] Leon E. Irish, Robert Kushen, and Karla W. Simon, *Guidelines for Laws Affecting Civic Organizations* (New York: Open Society Institute, 2004), p. 36.

[72] US State Department, Bureau of Democracy, Human Rights, and Labor, "Country Reports on Human Rights Practices – 2010: Bahrain" April 11, 2011, http://www.state.gov/j/drl/rls/hrrpt/2010/nea/154459.htm (accessed October 9, 2012).

[73] In addition to the cases of the Bahrain Youth Society for Human Rights and the Bahrain al-Nazaha Society, the Ministry of Social Development refused to register the Kindergarten Association in 2010. Al-Salam Society for Human Rights which

In the first two cases, the Ministry of Social Development in 2005 refused to register the Bahrain Youth Society for Human Rights (BYSHR) and in 2009 rejected the application of the Bahrain al-Nazaha Society. In the case of the Bahrain Human Rights Watch Society, the ministry ordered it to disband a coalition advocating women's rights.[74] The fourth example looks at the ministry's attempt to shut down a shelter managed by the Migrant Workers Protection Society.

1. Bahrain Youth Society for Human Rights

The Bahrain Youth Society for Human Rights (BYSHR), founded by a group of young rights activists, submitted its registration application in March 2005. According to one founder, Muhammad al-Maskati, the ministry never responded to the request, effectively rejecting the application to operate legally.[75]

The society nevertheless openly carried out activities, including public events and workshops. In February 2007, the ministry filed a complaint with the Public Prosecution, which then filed a case against al-Maskati on charges of "operating an organization without license."[76] Al-Maskati told Human Rights Watch that the ministry complained because "our work, activities, and cooperation with international rights groups increased."

> I believe this advocacy drew the attention of authorities and they wanted us
> to stop. The public prosecutor summoned me. During the questioning the
> officers asked about our work with international rights groups and human
> rights complaints we had sent to different UN agencies.[77]

According to the US State Department, the Ministry of Social Development rejected BYSHR's registration application "allegedly because of its ties to the dissolved Bahrain Center for Human Rights (BCHR) and because some of its members were younger than the

---

applied for registration in 2009 never received a response from the Ministry of Social Development, according to Hadi al-Mousawi, one of the founders.

74 Bahrain Human Rights Watch Society has no relationship whatsoever with Human Rights Watch and has frequently advocated positions reflecting the views of the government of Bahrain.

75 Human Rights Watch phone conversation with Muhammad al-Maskati, president of Bahrain Youth Society for Human Rights, August 3, 2012.

76 "The case of al-Maskati adjourned for closing argument, (تأجيل قضية المسقطي للمرافعة)," *Al-Wasat*, September 25, 2009, http://www.alwasatnews.com/2576/news/read/312663/1.html (accessed May 16, 2012).

77 Human Rights Watch, phone conversation with Muhammad al-Maskati, president of Bahrain Youth Society for Human Rights, August 3, 2012.

18 [years old]."[78] Al-Maskati told Human Rights Watch that he was the youngest among the founders and that he was 18 when the group applied for registration. He agreed that his ties with the BCHR might have been a factor:

> I think that they rejected the registration because of me. Before we started BYHRS I was actively involved with the Bahrain Center for Human Rights. When authorities filed the complaint they only targeted me, although there were many others working with BYHRS.[79]

On April 5, 2010, a minor criminal court fined al-Maskati 500 Bahraini Dinars (US$1,320) for operating an unlicensed organization.[80] On December 23, 2010, the Court of Appeal upheld the minor court's ruling and al-Maskati paid the fine.[81]

The society still monitors human rights violation in Bahrain and publishes news releases and reports. Al-Maskati told Human Rights Watch that authorities continue to harass the group. On October 16, 2012, security forces arrested al-Maskati on charges of participating in "illegal gathering" in Manama a week earlier. He was released on bail the following day.[82]

2. Bahrain al-Nazaha Society

On November 1, 2009, a group of journalists submitted an application to register the Bahrain al-Nazaha (Integrity) Society. According to its bylaws, the society's goal was to monitor elections at the municipal and national levels and internal civil society organization elections.

---

[78] US State Department, Bureau of Democracy, Human Rights, and Labor, "Country Reports on Human Rights Practices – 2009: Bahrain" March 11, 2010, http://www.state.gov/j/drl/rls/hrrpt/2009/nea/136066.htm (accessed October 9, 2012).

[79] Human Rights Watch, phone conversation with Muhammad al-Maskati, August 3, 2012. As noted earlier, authorities closed down the Bahrain Center for Human Rights in 2004.

[80] "Court fines al-Maskati 500 Dinars for establishing an unlicensed society, (القضاء يغرّم المسقطي 500 دينار لإنشائه جمعية غير مرخصة)," Al-Wasat, April 6, 2010, http://www.alwasatnews.com/2769/news/read/393925/1.html (accessed May, 16, 2012). In Bahrain's judicial system, misdemeanors are referred to minor criminal courts and felonies to high criminal courts.

[81] "Upholding a fine of 500 Dinars against al-Maskati for establishing an unlicensed society, (تأييد تغريم المسقطي 500 دينار لإنشائه جمعية غير مرخصة)," Al-Wasat, December 24, 2010, http://www.alwasatnews.com/3031/news/read/516689/1.html (accessed May 16, 2011).

[82] "Activist Muhammad al-Maskati released, (إخلاء سبيل الناشط محمد المسقطي)," Al-Wasat, October 18, 2012, http://www.alwasatnews.com/3694/news/read/709637/1.html (accessed April 1, 2013).

The ministry did not respond within 60 days of receiving the application, effectively rejecting the application. The group appealed to the ministry, which again did not respond within the 60 day period, thus reaffirming its denial of the application.[83] Hussain Mansour, one of the founders, told Human Rights Watch that the group had no choice but to resort to courts, "The ministry kept procrastinating and never responded to our letters. It became clear to us that the ministry didn't want to register our organization."[84]

On May 13, 2010, the group filed a lawsuit at the High Civil Court appealing the ministry's denial. On June 17, 2010, the ministry provided a written statement of the reason for its refusal to register the organization. The letter, signed by Najwa Janahi, director of NGO affairs in the ministry, said implausibly that "among the purposes of this association is achieving social goals, therefor the Ministry of Culture and Information is the specialized authority to register this association."[85] As noted, the law designates the Ministry of Information as the relevant authority solely for groups pursuing cultural and artistic goals.

The ministry also told the court that because the association goals included "spreading the culture of integrity," "supporting the Bahraini 2030 economic vision," "drafting an integrity code of conduct," and "monitoring ... referendums and elections," it fell outside the social development ministry's authority and that the founders should therefore seek to register with the Ministry of Information.[86] Mansour told Human Rights Watch that in court ministry officials argued that one of the stated missions of the organization, to "promote the culture of integrity," meant that it did not fall under the mandate of the social development ministry but rather the Ministry of Information.[87]

On April 26, 2011, the court agreed with the Ministry of Social Development that the "main goal of the association... was spreading the culture of integrity and [drafting] an integrity

---

[83] "Case of establishing al-Nazaha Society by a group of journalists adjourned, (إرجاء قضية إنشاء جمعية نزاهة من قبل مجموعة صحافيين)," Al-Wasat, May 6, 2012, http://www.alwasatnews.com/3529/news/read/660974/1.html (accessed May 18, 2012).

[84] Human Rights Watch, phone conversation with Hussain Mansour, 2012.

[85] Ministry of Social Development letter to founding members of the Bahrain al-Nazaha Society, June 17, 2010, copy is on file with Human Rights Watch.

[86] Defense Memorandum of the Ministry of Social Development to the High Civil Court, December 5, 2010, Copy is on file with Human Rights Watch. Human Rights Watch, phone conversation with Hussain Mansour, October 31, 2012. Also see: "Case of establishing al-Nazaha Society by a group of journalists adjourned, (إرجاء قضية إنشاء جمعية نزاهة من قبل مجموعة صحافيين)," Al-Wasat, May 6, 2012, http://www.alwasatnews.com/3529/news/read/660974/1.html (accessed May 18, 2012).

[87] Human Rights Watch, phone conversation with Hussain Mansour, October 31, 2012.

code of conduct," and that therefore the founders should seek to register with the Ministry of Information.[88] An appeals court upheld the ruling on June 25, 2012.[89] Mansour believes there were other reasons for rejecting the application:

> Our stated mission included organizing forums and lectures to discuss issues on integrity and combating corruption. I think authorities just did not want to register another rights organization that might challenge or criticize them.[90]

Mansour provided Human Rights Watch with a copy of the Ministry of Social Development's November 2011 decision to approve the registration of an association that focused on "spreading the culture of human rights" in its mission statement.

"The goal of both organizations was 'spreading a culture of something' but I believe the other organization was approved because the founders were pro-government supporters and ours was rejected because we were not considered government supporters," Mansour said.[91] Mansour said that he did not seek to register the organization with the Ministry of Information.

3. Bahrain Human Rights Watch Society

The Bahrain Human Rights Watch Society (BHRWS) was established in December 2004 by Faisal Fulad, then a member of the Shura Council, and 12 others.[92] The organization worked on several campaigns on migrant labor rights and frequently took positions on other human rights issues supporting the government. The group's first problem with authorities came after it established, along with the National Coalition to Stop Violence Against Women, the Respect Movement, in December 2005 to urge the government to draft a codified family law and protect domestic workers against abuse. The Ministry of Social Development effectively disbanded the coalition in July 2006 by requiring that the

---

[88] "Verdict in High Court of Appeal, first district, Case No. 17/2011/1706/1, June 25, 2012. Section on the ruling on the High Civil Court, Case No. 02/2010/5088/2, April 26, 2011. Copy on file with Human Rights Watch.

[89] Verdict in High Court of Appeal, first district, Case No. 17/2011/1706/1, June 25, 2012. Copy on file with Human Rights Watch.

[90] Human Rights Watch, phone conversation with Hussain Mansour, a founder of Bahrain al-Nazaha Society, October 31, 2012.

[91] Ibid.

[92] The Bahrain Human Rights Watch Society is not affiliated in any manner with Human Rights Watch.

coalition register as an NGO. Following the ministry's obstruction the BHRWS operated the campaign alone.[93]

4. Migrant Workers Protection Society

The Migrant Workers Protection Society (MWPS) was established in February 2005 to "educate the community about issues [facing] migrant workers" and "assist and protect the migrant workers."[94] The organization established a shelter in April 2005 for runaway female domestic workers.[95]

In August 2010, the Ministry of Social Development informed the MWPS that the society's shelter was not legally registered and must close. This followed an incident in which a migrant domestic worker fled to the shelter from the home of a high ministry official, claiming she had been abused.

The society successfully contested the ministry's effort to shut the shelter by providing a copy of the government's 2005 authorization of the shelter and noting that in previous years the ministry had donated funds to support the shelter.[96]

Takeover and Dissolution of NGOs

Civil society organizations that manage to register in Bahrain remain vulnerable to government takeover or arbitrary dissolution for violating such vague prohibitions as "engaging in politics" or—in the case of one organization—"serving [only] a certain segment of the society." Faced with arbitrary enforcement of vaguely worded laws, it is often simply a matter of time before groups that criticize government policies find themselves targeted by the authorities.

---

93 US State Department, Bureau of Democracy, Human Rights, and Labor, "Country Reports on Human Rights Practices – 2006: Bahrain" March 6, 2007, http://www.state.gov/j/drl/rls/hrrpt/2006/78850.htm (accessed October 9, 2012).

94 The Migrant Workers Protection Society, http://www.mwpsbahrain.com/index.html (accessed October 24, 2012).

95 US State Department, Bureau of Democracy, Human Rights, and Labor, "Country Reports on Human Rights Practices – 2010: Bahrain" April 11, 2011, http://www.state.gov/j/drl/rls/hrrpt/2010/nea/154459.htm (accessed October 9, 2012).

96 Human Rights Watch, World Report 2011 (New York: Human Rights Watch, 2011), Bahrain chapter, http://www.hrw.org/world-report-2011/world-report-2011-bahrain.

Current Law

Under the 1989 Law of Associations, the Ministry of Social Development can dismiss the officers and dissolve the board of directors of a group, and appoint ministry officials to run the group for up to one year.[97] In addition, the ministry can cancel results of elections for officers and boards of directors if authorities consider that the election violated the association's bylaws or the Law of Associations.[98] Article 50 enables the ministry to permanently dissolve or temporarily close organizations if the group is "unable to achieve its aims," or violates "the law, public order and norms."[99]

Draft Law

Under article 20 of the 2012 Law of Associations, the Minister of Social Development can take over a group in vaguely specified or trivial circumstances.[100] The minister can then appoint an "ad-hoc committee composed of members of the federation to which the civic organization belongs" or a director or interim board of the minister's choice.[101] The draft law stipulates that the assigned administrator obtain the ministry's approval to call for an election "at least a month" before his or her assignment ends.

The draft legislation improves upon this element of the current law by giving the NGO a chance to correct alleged violations of the law and ministerial regulations.[102] The ministry however decides which violations are correctable and sets a time limit to correct them.

Under the draft legislation the Ministry of Social Development retains the authority to close any organization and then, within 60 days, seek its permanent dissolution by administrative court order if it determines that the organization committed violations. These violations include being "unable to achieve the purposes it was established for... or

---

[97] Law No 21/1989, article 23 states that the "specialized minister" can replace managers and boards of directors when "the number of the board of directors becomes less than the number needed for the legal quorum or if the general assembly doesn't convene for two consecutive years without a reason acceptable by the specialized administrative authority."

[98] Law No 21/1989, Art. 47.

[99] Ibid., art. 50.

[100] The circumstances are: a) if the members of board director was less than the number needed for the legal quorum and it was not possible to meet the legal quorum; b) It the general assembly did not hold meeting for two consecutive years without a justification that the minister accepts; c) if the organization committed a violation which requires taking this action and the minister didn't have another solution. Draft Law on Civil Organizations and Institutions, art. 20.

[101] Draft Law on Civil Organizations and Institutions, art. 20.

[102] Ibid., art. 58.

exceeded those purposes ... or provided its services on factional, sectarian, or racial basis," or if the organization violates the Law of Associations.[103]

The draft law says that the minister's decision takes effect as soon as "a registered written order" reaches the NGO. It also says that the "order shall be implemented by force if necessary."[104] The NGO has 15 days to appeal a closure order to an administrative court.[105]

Recommended Standards

The International Center for Not-for-Profit Law (ICNL), which provides information on international legal standards for civic organizations, says that granting the power to ministries and state agencies to dissolve NGOs will have a "chilling effect on the independence and activities of civic organizations" and recommends that the law provide other penalties—for example, fines specific to different types of violations.[106]

According to the ICNL, termination and dissolution of an NGO should be "the last resort" and "only for the most serious and blatant violations, and then, except in cases involving the most urgent threat of irreparable harm, only after the civic organization has been given an opportunity to correct its behavior and challenge the allegations." The ICNL also recommends that any decision to dissolve an organization should not be implemented until "the appeal is completed or the time for appeal has lapsed."[107]

The ICNL's view is that civil society organizations "are key participants in framing and debating issues of public policy" and they have the right to freely express their views on "state actions, and policies ... to criticize (or praise) state officials and candidates for political office."[108] This recommendation stands in contrast to the broadly worded prohibition in Bahrain's current and draft associations laws against any "involvement in politics."

---

[103] Ibid., art. 58 (1-7).

[104] Draft Law on Civil Organizations and Institutions, art. 58.

[105] Ibid., 58.

[106] Leon E. Irish, Robert Kushen, and Karla W. Simon, *Guidelines for Laws Affecting Civic Organizations* (New York: Open Society Institute, 2004), p 37.

[107] Ibid., p 37.

[108] Ibid., p 55.

Case Studies

The following cases illustrate how authorities have used provisions of the 1989 Law of Associations to harass and in some cases close down groups critical of the government or its policies. Such actions have resulted in some groups ceasing to exist, while others continue to work in the shadows, vulnerable to harassment and possible prosecution.

These experiences also illustrate the authorities' arbitrary and inconsistent interpretation of the term "involvement in politics." It appears that when groups support the government and its policies, authorities welcome their expression of political views while groups critical of the government face serious consequences.

1. Bahrain Human Rights Society

The Bahrain Human Rights Society (BHRS) was registered in May 2001, with a stated mission to use "peaceful and legal means to promote human rights" and "achieve dignity, justice and equality."[109]

In August 2010, two months ahead of Chamber of Deputies and municipal elections, authorities arrested leading opposition activists and charged 25 of them (including two in absentia) on charges such as attempting to change the political system—considered a terrorism charge. Those detained were denied access to lawyers and family visits and alleged they had been subjected to torture during interrogation.[110]

On August 28, Abdulla al-Derazi, then secretary general of BHRS, held a press conference in which he talked about denial of basic rights of detainees—including access to lawyers and family members and right to a fair trial—and said that the arrests amounted to "enforced disappearance."[111]

---

[109] "Bahrain Human Rights Society, Who are We, "Bahrain Human Rights Society, http://bhrs.org/Who_We_are.aspx (accessed December 1, 2012).

[110] Human Rights Watch, *No Justice in Bahrain: Unfair Trials in Military and Civilian Courts*, February 28, 2012, http://www.hrw.org/reports/2012/02/28/no-justice-bahrain-o. The trials started on October 28, 2010, but the king freed the 23 defendants on February 22, 2011, after mass protests broke out in Bahrain.

[111] "Al-Derazi: The cases of arrested suspects are similar to "enforced disappearance", (الدرازي: حالات القبض على المتهمين أشبه بـ الاختفاء القسري)," *Al-Wasat*, August 29, 2010, http://www.alwasatnews.com/2914/news/read/471970/1.html (accessed May 21, 2012).

On September 1, 2010, the Ministry of Social Development accused the BHRS of supporting only the country's Shi'a population. "The activities offered by human rights associations"—the statement said, clearly referring to the BHRS—"are confined to serving a certain segment of the citizens."[112]

A week later, on September 8, the ministry issued an order dissolving the BHRS board of directors and replacing al-Derazi with a ministry official to run the organization.[113] In addition to alleging that the society was not acting impartially, the ministry listed what it said were administrative "irregularities," including failure to call for a general assembly and alleged cooperation with unspecified "illegal entities."[114]

On September 22, Fatima al-Balooshi, minister of social development, claimed that her order came in response to "illegal activities, particularly secret unlicensed training courses in Bahrain offered to individuals from neighboring states."[115] Al-Balooshi also accused al-Derazi and BHRS board members of arranging the trainings and contacting the trainees and "hiding the whole issue from specialized authorities."[116] Her statement ignored the fact that her ministry had in fact authorized the training course in question, a monitoring workshop for human rights defenders in the Gulf region.[117]

A day after al-Balooshi's accusation against the BHRS, the Ministry of Interior announced that it had launched an investigation of individuals who had undergone "unlicensed

---

[112] "[The Ministry of Social] Development: Private associations limit their services to a particular segment, (التنمية: جمعيات أهلية تحصر خدماتها في فئة معينة)," *Al-Wasat,* September 2, 2010, http://www.alwasatnews.com/2918/news/read/472601/1.html (accessed May 18, 2012).

[113] Decree No. 63 of 2010 in regard to appointing an interim director to administer Bahrain Human Rights Society, signed by Minister of Social Development Fatima al-Balooshi, November 8, 2010. Copy of the decree is on file with Human Rights Watch.

[114] "Bahrain: Revoke Order Dissolving Rights Group's Board," Human Rights Watch, news release, September 9, 2010, http://www.hrw.org/news/2010/09/09/bahrain-revoke-order-dissolving-rights-groups-board.

[115] "Dr. al-Balooshi: Bahrain Society for Human Rights committed serious administrative violations of the law, (الدكتورة البلوشي: الجمعية البحرينية لحقوق الانسان ارتكبت مخالفات ادارية جسيمة تتعارض مع القانون)," *Bahrain News Agency,* September 22, 2010, http://www.bna.bh/portal/news/169694 (accessed May 21, 2012).

[116] "Dr. al-Balooshi: Bahrain Society for Human Rights committed serious administrative violations of the law, (الدكتورة البلوشي: الجمعية البحرينية لحقوق الانسان ارتكبت مخالفات ادارية جسيمة تتعارض مع القانون)," *Bahrain News Agency,* September 22, 2010, http://www.bna.bh/portal/news/169694 (accessed May 21, 2012).

[117] "World Report 2011: Bahrain" Human Rights Watch, World Report, http://www.hrw.org/world-report-2011/world-report-2011-bahrain.

training" through the BHRS and would take legal action against them.[118] The statement did not identify the individuals but said they were considered "persona non grata" in Bahrain.

Al-Derazi replied that the BHRS had complied with all relevant administrative regulations.[119]

In late September 2010, the Ministry of Social Development filed a lawsuit against the society, seeking a court order forcing al-Derazi and board members to hand over "all funds, records, books and documents" to the ministry official serving as interim director.[120] The society countered by filing a complaint at the high administrative court, arguing that the ministry's order was taken "without checking with the board members of the society about any irregularities or launching an investigation with the general assembly." The ministry's suit "was entirely founded on rumors and hearsay," the BHRS said.[121]

On February 9, 2011, just days before street protests rocked the country, the ministry and BHRS reached an agreement in which the society withdrew its complaint and the ministry agreed to appoint a BHRS board member as interim director pending new elections.[122] On July 23, 2011, al-Derazi was re-elected as secretary-general of the society.[123]

2. Bahrain Center for Human Rights

A group of rights activists founded the Bahrain Center for Human Rights (BCHR) in 2002 to promote human rights and document rights violations. Among the founders was Abd al-Hadi al-Khawaja, who returned to Bahrain in June 2001 after spending 12 years in exile.

---

[118] "Ministry of Interior takes action against individuals who received courses and programs secretly through the Bahrain Society for Human Rights, (وزارة الداخلية بصدد اتخاذ إجراءات بحق الأشخاص الذين تلقوا دورات وبرامج سرّا من خلال الجمعية البحرينية لحقوق الإنسان)," *Bahrain News Agency* September 23, 2010, http://www.bna.bh/portal/news/169742?date=2012-03-28 (accessed May 21, 2012).

[119] "Bahrain: Revoke Order Dissolving Rights Group's Board," Human Rights Watch news release, September 9, 2010, http://www.hrw.org/news/2010/09/09/bahrain-revoke-order-dissolving-rights-groups-board.

[120] "The [Social] Development [Ministry] cancels its lawsuit against the Society for Human Rights, (التنمية تشطب دعواها ضد جمعية حقوق الإنسان)," *Al-Wasat*, October 12, 2010, http://www.alwasatnews.com/2958/news/read/483450/1.html (accessed May 18, 2012).

[121] "The Bahrain for Human Rights: The decision of the Development violates Associations Law and the International Covenant, (البحرينية لحقوق الإنسان: قرار التنمية مخالف لأحكام قانون الجمعيات والعهد الدولي)," *Al-Wasat*, October 8, 2010, http://www.alwasatnews.com/2954/news/read/482793/1.html (accessed May 18, 2012).

[122] "The [Ministry of Social] Development and the Bahraini for Human Rights reach amicable settlement, (التنمية والبحرينية لحقوق الإنسان تتوصلان إلى تسوية ودية)," *Al-Wasat*, February 10, 2011, http://www.alwasatnews.com/3079/news/read/526373/1.html (accessed May 18, 2012).

[123] On November 30, 2011 Al-Derazi resigned and in February 2012 the society elected Salman Kemal al-Din as secretary general. "Al-Derazi elected secretary general of the Bahraini for Human Rights and al-Gayeb as his deputy, (الدرازي أميناً عاماً لـ البحرينية لحقوق الإنسان والغانب نائباً له)," *Al-Wasat*, July 24, 2011, http://www.alwasatnews.com/3242/news/read/574015/1.html (accessed May 21, 2012).

On September 24, 2004, the BCHR organized a forum on poverty and economic rights at al-'Uruba Club. Al-Khawaja, then BCHR president, criticized Prime Minister Khalifa bin Salman Al Khalifa for his economic policies and alleged corrupt practices and human rights violations. A few days after the event, authorities closed the club and arrested al-Khawaja. Authorities allowed the club to re-open after 28 days.[124] On September 27, the Ministry of Labor and Social Affairs issued an order dissolving the BCHR, saying that it had committed "actions that are inconsistent with the Law of Associations of 1989 and the bylaws of the society," but not specifying which actions.[125] On November 21, 2004 a minor criminal court convicted al-Khawaja on charges of "inciting hatred against the regime" and sentenced him to one-year imprisonment. Just hours after the court ruling, King Hamad bin Isa Al Khalifa issued a decree pardoning him.[126]

The BCHR challenged the ministry's decision to dissolve the organization in court, but in February 2005 the High Civil Court confirmed the order. In June 2005, a court of appeal upheld the ruling.[127]

The BCHR has continued to operate, though authorities closed its office, confiscated its funds, and frequently harassed BCHR activists. On September 1, 2010, the pro-government daily *Al Watan* featured a front-page article alleging that Nabeel Rajab, who became president of BCHR in 2006, and al-Khawaja, who was then a regional protection coordinator for the Dublin-based Frontline organization, were linked to a "terrorist network" responsible for attacking persons and property, as well as plotting to carry out sabotage.[128]

Attacks against the BCHR intensified after the political unrest of 2011. In May 2012, authorities detained BCHR president Nabeel Rajab for allegedly "insulting" the Interior

---

[124] "Al-'Uruba opens its doors after 28 days of closure, (العروبة يفتح أبوابه بعد 28 يوماً من الإغلاق)," *Al-Wasat*, October 24, 2004, http://www.alwasatnews.com/779/news/read/418913/1.html (accessed May 22, 2012).

[125] "Government dissolves the Center for Human Rights… and Rajab: We will resort to court, (الحكومة تحل مركز حقوق الإنسان…. ورجب: سنلجأ إلى القضاء)," *Al-Wasat*, September 29, 2004, http://www.alwasatnews.com/754/news/read/413651/1.html (accessed May 22, 2012).

[126] "One year prison term for al-Khawaja… and release after hours, (السجن لمدة عام للخواجة… والإفراج عنه بعد ساعات)," *Al-Wasat*, November 22, 2004, http://www.alwasatnews.com/808/news/read/424124/1.html (accessed May 22, 2012).

[127] US State Department, Bureau of Democracy, Human Rights, and Labor, "Country Reports on Human Rights Practices – 2005: Bahrain" March 8, 2006, http://www.state.gov/j/drl/rls/hrrpt/2005/61686.htm (accessed October 9, 2012).

[128] Human Rights Watch, Letter to His Majesty Shaikh Hamad bin Isa Al Khalifa, September 3, 2010, http://www.hrw.org/news/2010/09/03/letter-his-majesty-shaikh-hamad-bin-isa-al-khalifa-regarding-torture-human-rights-ac.

Ministry and calling for the prime minister's resignation. At time of writing he was serving a two-year sentence after being convicted on charges of "illegal gathering."[129]

On December 17, 2012, security forces arrested Sayed Yusuf al-Muhafadha, acting vice-president of the BCHR, on charges of "willfully disseminating false news" after he posted a photo of an injured protester on his Twitter account. He was released on bail on January 17, 2013, and acquitted on March 11.[130]

3. Bahrain Teachers' Society

The Bahrain Teachers' Society (BTS) established in 2001 with a stated mission to advocate for the interests of teachers and defend their rights, has around 1,000 members comprising primary and secondary school teachers as well as university professors.

After five protesters died and hundreds were wounded when security forces responded with lethal force to peaceful demonstrations in mid-February 2011, many civil society organizations, among them the BTS, condemned the attacks.[131] The BTS also expressed concern for the safety of teachers and students in the aftermath of the clashes. Jalila al-Salman, BTS vice president, recalled:

> The first day of school after the mid-year break was going to be on February 20. After the incidents of February 14, teachers, students, and people were scared. Many people contacted us asking whether or not it was safe to go or send their children to school. We contacted the minister of education asking him to delay school, but he refused.[132]

---

[129] "Bahrain: Free Rights Activist Jailed for 'Illegal Gatherings,'" Human Rights Watch news release, August 16, 2012, http://www.hrw.org/news/2012/08/16/bahrain-free-rights-activist-jailed-illegal-gatherings.

[130] "Bahrain: Charges Against Rights Defender Raises Concerns", Human Rights Watch, news release, January 3, 2013, http://www.hrw.org/news/2013/01/03/bahrain-charges-against-rights-defender-raise-concerns. "Al-Mohafadha Acquitted of Broadcasting "False News" on Twitter, عبر تويتر "الأخبار الكاذبة" نشر تهمة من المحافظة تبرئة)," Al-Wasat, March 11, 2013, http://www.alwasatnews.com/3838/news/read/745665/1.html (accessed March 21, 2013). The public prosecution office appealed the ruling and a court of appeal will review the case in July 2013. Human Rights Watch online conversation with Sayed Yusuf al-Muhafadha, April 2, 2013.

[131] Between February 17 and March 23, 2011, the BTS issued 13 statements condemning the security forces' attacks on demonstrators and supported the protesters' demand for a constitutional monarchy. Copies of BTS's statements on file with Human Rights Watch.

[132] Human Rights Watch, interview with Jalila al-Salman, vice president of the Bahrain Teachers' Society, Manama, November 26, 2011.

On February 20, the BTS joined a general strike called for by the General Federation of Bahrain Trade Unions (GFBTU), which represents more than 70 trade unions in Bahrain, demanding that authorities withdraw security forces from streets and allow for peaceful demonstrations.[133]

As reports of assaults against protesting teachers and students circulated in late February, the BTS on March 2 called on Minister of Education Majid bin Ali al-Nuaimi to resign because of what BTS called "an aggressive campaign" targeting students and teachers.[134]

On March 11, as clashes between protesters and pro-government groups intensified, the society called on teachers to join a second GFBTU strike scheduled for March 13. [135] On March 12 Al-Mustaqleen (Independents), a pro-government parliamentary faction, called on the government "to investigate the Bahrain Teachers' Society ... and take legal measures to dissolve it ... because [BTS] is responsible for politicizing the educational process and spreading chaos and sectarian hatred within schools."[136]

On April 17, 2011, Abdulla al-Mtaw'a, under-secretary of the Ministry of Education, said on state-run Bahrain TV, "God afflicted us with a plague called the Bahrain Teachers' Society which has bet against the education process." He vowed to prosecute teachers and students who participated in the demonstrations.[137]

Beginning on March 14, 2011, Bahraini military and security forces arrested thousands of demonstrators and protest supporters, including BTS leaders and members. On March 23, the minister of education said the government would take legal action against the BTS:

---

[133] The BTS is not officially part of the GFBTU. According to al-Salman, more than 9,000 teachers (nearly 90 percent of all teachers) participated in the strike. The GFBTU's strike lasted one day but the teachers, led by BTS, continued to strike until February 24, 2012. For details of the GFBTU's strike, see: "Report of the Bahrain Independent Commission of Inquiry, November 23, 2011, para 1340.

[134] Statement Number 9, Bahrain Teachers' Society, March 2, 2011.

[135] Statement Number 11, Bahrain Teachers' Society, March 13, 2011; Statement issued by the General Federation of Bahrain Trade Unions, (بيان صادر عن الاتحاد العام لنقابات عمال البحرين); http://www.bhteachers.org/portal/news.php?action=view&id=60 (accessed May 24, 2012), On March 23 the BTS ended its strike and told teachers: "Everyone has the right to assess his situation and ... can take a decision that is suitable for him." Statement Number 13, Bahrain Teachers' Society, March 23, 2011.

[136] "Al-Mustaqleen calls for the dissolution of Teachers Society and prosecution of its leaders, (المستقلين تطالب بحل جمعية المعلمين ومحاكمة رموزها)," Al-Ayam, March 12, 2011, http://www.alayam.com/Articles.aspx?aid=70989 (accessed May 22, 2012).

[137] See https://www.youtube.com/watch?v=eq3EKuTNJkc (accessed October 23, 2012).

The society adopted political stances ... and it became an integral branch of a political [party] ... it has irregularities and we have called on the ministry [of social development] to review the registration of the society... We will also file a complaint with the Office of the Public Prosecution.[138]

On March 29, security forces arrested BTS Vice-President Jalila al-Salman in a pre-dawn raid on her home.[139] Regarding her interrogation, al-Salman told Human Rights Watch:

I was asked questions such as: "Why did you issue statements? What is your relationship with Iran? You want to break down the education [system]?"[140]

Security forces apprehended BTS President Mahdi Abu Deeb in a pre-dawn raid on the house of a relative on April 6. The same day the Ministry of Social Development dissolved the BTS, saying it had:

Issued inciting statements and speeches... to hold strikes... in addition to exploiting school students at all levels and spreading the concept of demonstration and creating chaos ... [Abu Deeb] gave a number of inciting speeches... which took on a political nature against the state system and deviated from the goals of the society.[141]

Seven BTS board members were also arrested but subsequently acquitted of charges that they had also incited crimes.[142]

---

[138] "Bahraini Minister of Education to Al-Sharq al-Awsat: We will not allow politicization of the educational system, (وزير التربية البحريني لـ الشرق الأوسط: لن نسمح بتسييس السلك التعليمي)," *Al-Sharq al-Awsat*, March 23, 2011, http://www.aawsat.com/details.asp?section=4&article=613830&issueno=11803 (accessed May 23, 2012).

[139] Al-Salman remained in jail until August 21; was re-arrested in a pre-dawn raid on October 18 and held for two more weeks; and once again arrested November 17, 2012 and held for 17 days. Human Rights Watch correspondence with Jalila al-Salman, December 6, 2012.

[140] Human Rights Watch interview with Jalila al-Salman, vice president of the Bahrain Teachers' Society, Manama, November 26, 2011.

[141] "Ministry of Social Development dissolves the Teachers Association and suspends the management board of the Medical Society, (وزارة التنمية الاجتماعية تحل جمعية المعلمين البحرينية وتوقف مجلس إدارة جمعية الأطباء)," *Bahrain News Agency*, April 6, 2011, http://www.bna.bh/portal/news/451949 (accessed December 6, 2011).

[142] "Acquittal for seven defendants of the Teachers' Society, (البراءة للمتهمين الـ 7 بقضية جمعية المعلمين)," *Al-Wasat*, March 27, 2012, http://www.alwasatnews.com/3489/news/read/645995/1.html (accessed May 25, 2012).

Abu Deeb and al-Salman each faced 12 charges, including two under provisions of the Law of Associations: "involvement in politics" (article 18), and failure to "work in line with the purpose of the association.... [and] spending assets of the association on activities that do not achieve the purpose of the association" (article 89[3]).[143]

On September 25, a special military court found Abu Deeb and al-Salman guilty and sentenced Abu Deeb to 10 years in prison and al-Salman to 3 years.[144]On October 21, a civilian court of appeal reduced Abu Deeb's sentence to five years and al-Salman's to six months.[145]The court of cassation had yet to review the verdict at time of writing.

4. Bahrain Nursing Society

The Bahrain Nursing Society (BNS), a professional association established in 1991 and registered with the Ministry of Social Development, has around 500 members. Its stated mission is to "defend the rights of nurses and spread the culture of health among the public."[146]

In March 2007, the general assembly amended some provisions of its bylaws and sought the approval of the Ministry of Social Development. The society also scheduled its general assembly for July 2007.

On July 3, 2007, an official informed the society that the ministry had "lost" the copy of the amendments and needed a second copy.[147] This was at a time when the society sought the ministry's approval to delay its board elections from July 1 to July 9, and to apply the proposed amendments which allowed only members with executive experience to nominate themselves to the board.

---

[143] Military Prosecution Office, Referral to National Safety Court, May, 25, 2011.

[144] Verdict in National Safety Court, Case No. 599/2011, September 25, 2011.

[145] At this writing Abu Deeb was still in prison. "Court Reduces Sentences of Teachers' Society Officers: Abu Deeb To Serve 5 years; Salman Receives 6 Months" Information Affairs Authority, October 21, 2012, http://iaa.bh/pressReleasedetails.aspx?id=375 (accessed October 22, 2012).

[146] Human Rights Watch, phone conversation with Ibrahim al-Dimistani, vice president of Bahrain Nursing Society, August 1, 2012.

[147] Verdict in High Civil Court, Case No. 02/2008/8983/8. The court document provides detail accounts of the correspondents between the Ministry of Social Development and the Bahrain Nursing Society, copy is on file with Human Rights Watch.

On August 27, the ministry said that the BNS could not operate with the new amendments until the ministry approved them and published the approval in the *Official Gazette*, the government's official newspaper. The society did not hold its general assembly meeting until November 14, 2007, which a ministry representative attended, but due to lack of a quorum the meeting adjourned to January 8, 2008.[148]

On January 8, the BNS general assembly decided to extend the tenure of the board of directors until the next elections. Muhammad al-Fardan from the Ministry of Social Development attended the meeting and "confirmed the legality of the decisions."[149]

In June 2008, the society launched a campaign demanding an increase in nurses' salaries and benefits. According to BNS president Rula al-Saffar, the campaign drew the unwanted attention of authorities:

> The campaign was something new and authorities were not happy with it. In the past, associations used to be shy to speak out about many issues that affected their members, but we came and peacefully demanded more rights for our members. Then authorities froze the bank account of the society and they either tried to discourage or scare nurses to abandon the campaign and encourage others to sue us.[150]

In July 2008, the Ministry of Social Development announced that BNS board of directors was "illegitimate" because the organization had failed to notify authorities about its general assembly meeting in January 2008 and had not "presented a record of its activities and [a copy of] its bylaws to the ministry."[151] Ibrahim al-Dimistani, the group's vice-president, said the group had "fax" evidence that the ministry had received all relevant documents.[152]

---

[148] Verdict in High Civil Court, Case No. 02/2008/8983/8.,copy on file with Human Rights Watch.

[149] Ibid.

[150] Human Rights Watch interview with Rula al-Saffar, Manama, November 26, 2011.

[151] "Al-Dimistani: The documents of the Nursing Society refutes the allegations of the Ministry of Social Development, (الدستاني: وثائق جمعية التمريض تدحض إدعاءات التنمية)," *Al-Waqt*, July 27, 2008, http://www.alwaqt.com/print.php?aid=124239 (accessed May 22 2012).

[152] Ibid.

On August 5, the society set August 24 to hold a new election. However, on August 11, the ministry unilaterally replaced al-Saffar with an interim director.[153] BNS board members rejected the appointed director.[154]

In August 2008, the public prosecution charged al-Saffar and al-Dimistani with "insulting and defaming" ministry of health officials, alleging that they had accused the officials of corruption in a newspaper interview. In April 2009, a court acquitted them of the charge.[155]

Despite the ministry's objection to the BNS August 2008 general assembly meeting and its dismissal of al-Saffar, the society held elections on August 26, 2008, and re-elected al-Saffar as president.[156]

In early September 2008, the Ministry of Social Development froze the BNS's bank account, preventing it from accessing its funds. On November 30, the ministry re-appointed the interim director and once again the BNS board refused to work with her.[157] The ministry then again referred the BNS to the Office of the Public Prosecution, alleging the elected board of directors was "illegitimate" and had violated "its bylaws and the Law of Associations."[158]

The society appealed the ministry's decision to appoint an interim director and the ministry's objection to the August 2008 general assembly meeting to the High Civil Court. On October 10, 2010, the court ruled the election legitimate. However the court upheld the appointment of an interim director.[159] In January 2010, according to al-Dimistani, an appeals court upheld the ruling.[160] In April 2012, the Court of Cassation upheld the ruling.[161]

---

153 Decree No. 32 of 2008 in regard to appointing an interim director to Bahrain Nursing Society, signed by Fatima al-Balooshi, minister of social development, and August 11, 2008. Copy of the decree is on file with Human Rights Watch.

154 The Public Prosecution Office later filed a lawsuit against al-Saffar and al-Dimistani charging them with having "performed the affairs of the society while they had been prohibited from doing so" when the ministry of Social Development appointed an interim director. In July 2011, the Second District Criminal Court sentenced al-Saffar and al-Dimistani to one month in prison. In December 2012 the Court of Appeal upheld the sentences. Authorities arrested al-Saffar but released her shortly afterwards because she had already served the time of her sentence after she was arrested in the government crackdown on demonstrations in March 2011. Human Rights Watch interview with Rula al-Saffar, Manama, November 26, 2011.

155 "Bahrain: De facto closure of the Bahrain Nursing Society," Front Line Defenders, March 26, 2010, http://www.frontlinedefenders.org/node/2426 (accessed October 22, 2012).

156 "Rula al-Saffar reserves the presidency of the Nursing, (رولا الصفار تحتفظ برئاسة التمريض)," Al-Wasat, August 27, 2008, http://www.alwasatnews.com/2182/news/read/164182/1.html (accessed May 22, 2012).

157 Decree No. 43 of 2008 in regard to renewing the appointment of an interim director to Bahrain Nursing Society, signed by Fatima al-Balooshi, minister of Social Development, November 30, 2008. Copy of the decree is on file with Human Rights Watch.

158 "The Ministry of Social Development prosecutes the [Bahrain] Nursing Society, (التنمية تقاضي جمعية التمريض...)," Al-Waqt, December 27, 2008, http://www.alwaqt.com/art.php?aid=144476 (accessed October 22, 2012).

159 The court said that the Bahrain Nursing Society violated article 23 of the Law of Associations (No 21/1989) by failing to hold the general assembly meeting for two consecutive years and that according to article 30 of the Law of Associations

The next confrontation came several months later. Authorities arrested al-Dimistani on March 17, 2010, after he allegedly provided medical treatment to a person who had been shot and wounded during an anti-government demonstration, accusing him of "hiding and harboring a fugitive."[162] Muhammad al-Tajir, al-Dimistani's lawyer, said that authorities did not formally charge him with any crime.[163] On March 23, 2010, a Ministry of Interior official telephoned al-Saffar, ordering her to cancel a party that she had planned to celebrate al-Dimistani's March 21 release on bail.[164]

A few hours after this phone call, security forces changed the lock on the doors of the BNS office inside the Salmaniya Medical Complex, effectively shutting down the organization.[165]

In April 2011, security forces again arrested al-Dimistani (April 3) and al-Saffar (April 4). They were among 20 doctors, nurses, and paramedics charged with forcibly taking over the Salmaniya Medical Complex and providing treatment to patients based on sectarian affiliation.[166] Both told Human Rights Watch that they were subjected to torture in detention. "I was handcuffed and blindfolded [and] interrogated for seven days," al-Saffar told Human Rights Watch.

> The interrogations started at 3:30 p.m. and went on until 5 or 6 a.m. the next day. I was electrocuted in my face and my head. They [threatened me, saying], "We are going to rape you." I was held in a very cold cell. They turned on the air conditioner, which made the cell even colder and I had no blanket. They forced me to stand and sit for long hours on the dirty floor. During the course of my interrogation [the officer] told me, "I have been waiting for you since 2008."[167]

Minister of Social Development had the authority to assign an interim. Verdict in High Civil Court, Case No. 02/2008/8983/8, copy on file with Human Rights Watch.

[160] Human Rights Watch, phone conversation with Ibrahim al-Dimistani, August 1, 2012.

[161] Verdict in Court of Cassation, appeal case No. 621/ 2010, Case No. 8983/2008.

[162] "Bahrain: Set Aside Ruling Against Activist," Human Rights Watch, news release, May 14, 2010, http://www.hrw.org/news/2010/05/14/bahrain-set-aside-ruling-against-activist.

[163] Human Rights Watch, online conversation with Muhammad al-Tajir, March 16, 2013.

[164] Human Rights Watch, interview with Rula al-Saffar, Manama, November 26, 2011.

[165] Human Rights Watch, phone conversation with Ibrahim al-Dimistani, August 1, 2012.

[166] "Bahrain: Medics Describe Torture in Detention," Human Rights Watch, news release, October 22, 2011, http://www.hrw.org/news/2011/10/21/bahrain-medics-describe-torture-detention.

[167] Human Rights Watch, phone conversation with Rula al-Saffar, October 10, 2011.

She and al-Dimistani were released on bail on August 21 and September 7, respectively. On September 23, 2011, a special military court sentenced al-Saffar and al-Dimistani each to 15 years in prison.[168] On June 14, 2012, a civilian court of appeals upheld the convictions of nine doctors and medical personnel, but reduced al-Dimistani's sentence to three years and overturned al-Saffar's conviction.[169] On October 1, the Court of Cassation affirmed al-Dimistani's conviction and his three-year sentence. Security forces took him into custody in an early morning raid on his home the next morning.[170] He remains in detention at the time of writing.

Despite the January 2010 appeals court ruling in favor of the BNS, the society's bank account remains frozen by the Ministry of Social Development.[171]

5. Bahrain Medical Society

Other organizations encountered similar problems with authorities in the wake of the February-March 2011 political crisis. On April 6, 2011, the Ministry of Social Development suspended the board of directors of the Bahrain Medical Society (BMS) and appointed an interim manager and board members.[172] The ministry claimed that the society had "depart[ed] from the goals that the society was founded for and engaged in politics."[173]

The ministry's decision came in response to statements of the BMS and the Bahrain Dental Society during the anti-government demonstrations. On February 17, the two organizations condemned security forces' excessive use of force and "preventing health workers from providing care to the injured."[174] Two days later, the organizations jointly criticized a

---

[168] "The Military Prosecutor states verdicts," *Bahrain News Agency*, September 29, 2011, http://bna.bh/portal/en/news/474663?date=2011-09-29 (accessed August 25, 2012)

[169] "Bahrain: Court Upholds Convictions of Medics," Human Rights Watch, news release, June 14, 2012, http://www.hrw.org/news/2012/06/15/bahrain-court-upholds-convictions-medics.

[170] "Bahrain: King Should Quash Convictions," Human Rights Watch, news release, October 8, 2012, http://www.hrw.org/news/2012/10/08/bahrain-king-should-quash-convictions.

[171] Human Rights Watch, phone conversation with Rula al-Saffar, October 10, 2011.

[172] Ministry of Social Development dissolves the Teachers Association and suspends the management board of the Medical Society, (وزارة التنمية الاجتماعية تحل جمعية المعلمين البحرينية وتوقف مجلس إدارة جمعية الأطباء)," *Bahrain News Agency*, April 6, 2011, http://www.bna.bh/portal/news/451949 (accessed December 6, 2011).

[173] "Ministry of Social Development dissolves the Teachers Association and suspends the management board of the Medical Society, (وزارة التنمية الاجتماعية تحل جمعية المعلمين البحرينية وتوقف مجلس إدارة جمعية الأطباء)," *Bahrain News Agency*, April 6, 2011, http://www.bna.bh/portal/news/451949 (accessed December 6, 2011).

[174] "Urgent Press Release from the Bahrain Medical Society and the Bahrain Dental Society, (بيان طارئ جمعية الأطباء البحرينية) (وجمعية أطباء الفم والأسنان البحرينية)," *Al-Wasat*, February 17, 2011, http://www.alwasatnews.com/3086/news/read/527745/1.html (accessed May 21, 2012).

statement of the minister of health asserting that the "number of wounded [on February 18] was only seven minor injuries." The organizations said that the actual number of casualties that day exceeded 100.[175]

Under the appointed director, Nabeel al-Ansari, the BMS made a complete volte-face. The new board issued a statement expressing "full allegiance to the nation and [its] leadership" and "deploring the recent incidents and the violations made by BMS's previous board of directors."[176] Al-Ansari called the detained doctors and medical personnel "traitors."[177]

On April 13, 2012, a year after the government's takeover, the BMS held new elections for president and board members. Several candidates withdrew from the election to protest a decision by the appointed board allowing non-Bahraini physicians to vote in the election, which they said enabled the government-supported candidates to win.[178] BMS bylaws specify that only Bahraini nationals can vote in the general assembly.[179] The day before the election, Minister of Social Development Fatima al-Balooshi declared that "the participation of the foreign doctors in the society's election is their natural right because they are serving this country."[180]

---

[175] "Second Statement of the Bahrain Medical Society and the Bahrain Dental Society, (و جمعية الأطباء البحرينية :البيان الثاني (جمعية أطباء الفم والأسنان البحرينية)," *Al-Wasat*, February 19, 2012, http://www.alwasatnews.com/3088/news/read/528059/1.html (accessed May 21, 2012).

[176] "BMS denounces recent incidents in Bahrain" *Bahrain News Agency*, April 21, 2012, http://www.bna.bh/portal/en/news/453772?date=2011-05-12 (accessed May 18, 2012).

[177] "Irish delegation to Manama attacked by Bahrain Medical Society chairman," *Irish Central*, July 13, 2011, http://www.irishcentral.com/news/Irish-delegation-to-Manama-attacked-by-Bahrain-Medical-Society-chairman-125712258.html (accessed October 22, 2012).

[178] Following the arrests and dismissals of numerous Bahraini doctors and other medical personnel the government recruited medical personnel from abroad. See: Department of Foreign Affairs [Philippines]: Bahrain wants to hire Pinoy medical workers, GMA News (a Philippines news network), May 10, 2011, http://www.gmanetwork.com/news/story/220151/pinoyabroad/dfa-bahrain-wants-to-hire-pinoy-medical-workers, (accessed, April 2, 2013) Dr. Taha al-Dirazi, a candidate, said told *Al-Wasat* that the Bahrain Medical Society had 439 eligible voters but at the 2012 elections the number of eligible voters spiked to 872. "Candidates for the presidency of Medical Society confirm the management committed violations, (مرشحون لرئاسة جمعية الأطباء يؤكدون ارتكاب الإدارة المعيَّنة مخالفات)," *Al-Wasat*, April 12, 2012, http://www.alwasatnews.com/3505/news/read/655345/1.html (accessed May 21, 2012).

[179] Bahrain Medical Society bylaws, arts. 9 and 10 (A).

[180] "Al-Balooshi to Al-Watan: Politicization of the Medical election is possible and the participation of the foreigners is a natural right (البلوشي لـالوطن: تسييس انتخابات الأطباء وارد ومشاركة الأجنبي حق طبيعي)," *Al-Watan*, April 12, 2012, http://www.alwatannews.net/news.aspx?id=ZaQK8d62FX/kZzxK+ChA7Q== (accessed May 22, 2012).

Dr. Jalal al-Mousawi, a candidate for BMS vice-president, told Human Rights Watch why he withdrew: "We just could not compete in the election because unlike previous elections, we, independents and opposition, suddenly became the minority."[181]

On May 21, a group of BMS members sought an administrative court order to freeze the elected board and hold a new election.[182] The ministry defended allowing non-Bahrainis to vote in the election, saying that it had launched a "comprehensive review" to determine to what extent Bahrain complies with international human rights treaties, namely the ICCPR. The ministry said it found "an explicit difference between the memberships of citizens and non-citizens, which contradicts with provisions of some treaties that Bahrain has ratified."[183] The BMS members noted that Bahrain ratified the ICCPR in 2006 but the ministry never previously expressed concern about the BMS's bylaws.[184] At time of writing the High Civil Court was reviewing the case.[185]

6. Bahrain Lawyers' Society

The Bahrain Lawyers' Society (BLS), the official professional body for lawyers in Bahrain, was established in 1977 and today has about 200 members. The society publicly criticized the Ministry of Social Development's decisions to suspend the board of directors of the Bahrain Human Rights Society in September 2010, to replace the president of Bahrain Nursing Society in August 2008, and to dissolve the Bahrain Center for Human Rights in September 2004.[186]

Authorities moved against the BLS on two occasions. In 1998, the Ministry of Labor and Social Development, then in charge of civil society groups, suspended its board of directors because it had allegedly "engaged in political activities"—an apparent reference

---

[181] Human Rights Watch, telephone conversation with Dr. Jalal al-Mousawi, Manama, May 22, 2012.

[182] Ibid.

[183] Defense Memorandum of the Ministry of Social Development, High Civil Court, Case No. 2012/7873, copy on file with Human Rights Watch.

[184] Ibid.

[185] On March 31, 2013, the court ordered the BMS to provide a list member who had attended election on April 13, 2012 to determine if there were non-Bahraini among them as well is doctors who are members of other organizations. High Civil Court, Case No. 02/2012/7873/5, March 31, 2013. Copy on file with Human Rights Watch.

[186] "Hilal calls on the Ministry of Development to cancel its decision to reinstate former board of Lawyers, (بالغاء هلال يطالب التنمية) (قرارها بتعيين الإدارة السابقة لـ المحامين)," Al-Wasat, December 11, 2011, http://alwasatnews.com/3382/news/print/614108/1.html (accessed December 16, 2011).

to a seminar that the society had hosted in January 1998.[187] The society appealed the decision and administrative court ruled in favor of the society.

In an October 26, 2011 letter to the society, the Ministry of Social Development asked for documentation to verify the society's membership records.[188] On November 30, the minister of social development canceled by decree the board election results of November 26 and reinstated the previous board and president to manage the affairs of the society. Saying that the society "did not comply with legal procedures," the ministry also froze the society's bank account, according to the newly elected BLS president Hamid al-Mullah.[189]

Al-Mullah said that the BLS in fact notified the ministry about the November meeting and the election two weeks before they were held. "The ministry refused to accept the notification letter when we tried to deliver it in person," he said, "so we sent it via registered mail and received delivery confirmation."[190]

> We [didn't] have all those documents because some of them date back to 1977, when the society was founded. The ministry has been supervising all elections and the society has sent membership lists before every election. They probably have those documents.[191]

On December 25, in response to a Human Rights Watch statement criticizing the action, the ministry claimed that the society had failed to inform the ministry and provide it with an updated list of its members before holding the November 2011 general assembly.[192]

In late 2011, al-Mullah sought a court order to void the ministry's November 30 appointment of an interim board.[193] Sayed Mohsin al-Alawi, BLS director of culture and

---

[187] "Bar Association Confiscated In Bahrain, (مصادرة جمعية المحامين البحرينية)," Arab Commission For Human Rights, November 1998, http://www.achr.nu/rep14.htm (accessed August 1, 2012).

[188] Copy of the ministry's correspondence with Bahrain Lawyers' Society on file with Human Rights Watch.

[189] Decree No. 57 of 2011 in regard to cancelling the general assembly of Bahrain Lawyers' Society, signed by Fatima al-Balooshi, minister of Social Development, November 30, 2011. Human Rights Watch, telephone conversation with Hamid al-Mullah, October 25, 2012.

[190] Human Rights Watch, telephone conversation with Hamid al-Mullah, December 19, 2011.

[191] Ibid.

[192] Ministry of Social Development, Statement in response to Human Rights Watch Statement, December 20, 2011.

[193] Human Rights Watch, telephone conversation with Hameed al-Mullah, elected president of the Bahrain Lawyers' Society, December 19, 2011.

media, told Human Rights Watch that after the six-month term of the interim board ended in May 2012, the board elected in November 2011 took charge of the affairs of the society.[194]

According to court records the society argued that as long as a member paid membership fees "even just before holding the general assembly" they could vote and nominate themselves. The High Civil Court disagreed, and on October 24, 2012, ruled in favor of the ministry, saying that "there were violations in regard to some members who had the right to vote and nominate... more than one member paid different membership fees... some of those members had not paid membership fees for more than a year, some more than five years and others 10 years."[195] The society was appealing the ruling at time of writing.

NGO Funding

Groups in Bahrain have two main sources of funding: membership fees and government funds for NGO activities that the Ministry of Social Development approves.[196] Sometimes these funds do not cover operations, and some groups have a policy not to accept government funds.[197] As a result, some groups look for alternative sources of income, such as donations by individuals and foreign grants. Bahraini laws and regulations do not prohibit, but do significantly curtail, soliciting and receiving foreign funds.

Current Law

Article 21 of the 1989 Law of Associations says that groups must obtain written permission from a "specialized minister"—in the case of most NGOs, the minister of social development—to undertake fundraising.[198] The law gives the minister the authority to dissolve organizations if they acquire money from, or send money to, a party outside Bahrain without written permission.[199]

---

[194] Human Rights Watch, telephone conversation with Sayed Mohsin al-Alawi, August 8, 2012.

[195] Human Rights Watch, telephone conversation with Hamid al-Mullah, October 25, 2012.

[196] Human Rights Watch meeting with Khalid al-Koheji, assistant under-secretary for community affairs, who is responsible for nongovernmental groups, Sultan Hammadi, the ministry's legal counselor for nongovernmental group affairs, Manama, February 27, 2013.

[197] Among those that do not accept government funds are the Bahrain Center for Human Rights and Bahrain Youth Society for Human Rights.

[198] Law No 21/1989, arts. 21, 22.

[199] Law No 21/1989, arts 20.

In January 2006, Minister of Social Development Fatima al-Balooshi issued Ministerial Decree No. 27 stating that fundraising licenses are valid only for two months, and that the funds sought must be "linked to an activity that will be held at a specified time and date or for a special occasion or to cope with urgent circumstances." Groups must inform the ministry how they will collect the money, the name and number of the bank account, and how they will spend the funds. If the ministry does not respond favorably within 30 days, the request is considered to be denied.[200] Under article 9 of the decree, associations must record the name of every donor, eliminating any chance for anonymous donations.[201] Article 14 grants the Ministry of Social Development power to "confiscate [funds] and distribute [them] to social activities" it favors if it considers the organization in question to have violated conditions laid out by the ministry in the fundraising license.[202]

Draft Law

The 2012 Draft Law of Associations says that organizations can accept donations and raise funds after receiving "written permission" from the Ministry of Social Development and in accordance with the executive regulations of the law.[203] The draft law permits groups to own property and make investments "to a necessary extent" provided that they are intended to advance the organization's goals and are not intended for profit. The organizations must inform the ministry about any such investments.[204]

Recommended Standards

Any regulation of NGOs should focus on their conduct, not their source of funds. So long as an organization is engaged in peaceful advocacy, including critical dissent, it should be entitled to do so as a matter of right, regardless of who funds it.[205] The law should allow for the receipt of donations or contributions from foreign donors as long as all foreign exchange and customs laws are satisfied and make all criteria for restrictions transparent.

---

[200] "Decree No. 27/2006 ((2006 /27 قانون رقم)" art. 3 (4), (5), (6), (7).

[201] "Decree No. 27/2006 ((2006 /27 قانون رقم)" art. 9.

[202] "Decree No. 27/2006 ((2006 /27 قانون رقم)" art. 14.

[203] Draft Law on Civil Organizations and Institutions, art. 17. It was unclear at the time of writing if the executive regulations pertaining to the existing Law 89 (Decree No. 27 of 2006) would also apply once the draft law goes into effect.

[204] Draft Law on Civil Organizations and Institutions, art. 18.

[205] Kenneth Roth, "Egypt's NGO Funding Crackdown," *Foreign Policy*, April 9, 2013, http://mideast.foreignpolicy.com/posts/2013/04/09/egypt_s_ngo_funding_crackdown (accessed May 29, 2013).

The International Center for Non-for-Profit Law suggests that a requirement to secure a license for fundraising "might not be problematic on its own," but requiring multiple applications constitutes a "burdensome and expensive administrative process."[206] It recommends that groups "be permitted to engage in all legally acceptable and culturally appropriate fundraising activities" and that registration should be required only when the fundraising is "through a public solicitation."[207]

The Open Society Institute's *Guidelines for Laws Affecting Civic Organizations* argues that registered NGOs should "be allowed to receive cash or in-kind donations, transfers, or loans from sources outside the country so long as all generally applicable foreign exchange and customs laws are satisfied."[208]

---

[206] Global Trends in NGO Law, the International Center for Not-for-Profit Law, vol. 1, issue 4, Survey of Arab NGO Law, March 2010 p. 9.

[207] "Checklist for NGO Laws," International Center for Not-for-Profit Law.

[208] Leon E. Irish, Robert Kushen, and Karla W. Simon, *Guidelines for Laws Affecting Civic Organizations* (New York: Open Society Institute, 2004), p. 89.

بعضهم موظف في وزارتي «الصحة»، و«التربية»، ومعهد التدريب

«الوطن» تكشف قائمة المشاركين بتشويه سمعة البحرين في جنيف

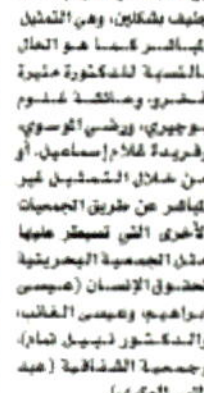

- المشاركون حاولوا تشويه السمعة الحقوقية للمملكة ومازالوا خارج المساءلة
- 10 منظمات ساهمت في تشويه السمعة تدعمها 4 أجنبية
- 19 شخصاً لا يعملون فمن الذي مولهم للمشاركة في جنيف؟!

On September 18, 2012, Bahraini civil society leaders and political activists attended the 21st session of the UN Human Rights Council in Geneva where they held side-events to spotlight Bahrain's human rights record.

Pro-government media slammed them for "distorting" the image of Bahrain. *Al-Watan*'s September 23, 2012 edition of *Al-Watan* included a full-page article with a headline that read: "*Al-Watan* discloses the list of those who participated in distorting Bahrain's image in Geneva." Accompanying the article were photos of 34 of the activists.

"Public demand is growing to hold accountable individuals who participated in distorting Bahrain's image at the end of Human Rights Council's session," the newspaper asserted, citing calls by Shura Council members "reaffirming that anyone who distorts his country's image is a traitor and does not deserve to carry its citizenship."

III. Political Societies

In 2005 King Hamad signed the Law for Political Societies (Law No. 26/2005). Political parties remain prohibited but today 20 licensed political societies operate in the country, including Islamist and secular, pro-government, and opposition groups.[209]

This section analyzes the laws that regulate political societies in Bahrain and presents case studies that show how authorities have used these laws to regulate their right to freedom of association, expression, and peaceful assembly. Other laws, such as the Public Gathering Law of 1973 and the Press Law of 2002, also unduly restrict the activities of political societies as they relate to freedom of assembly and expression.

Legal Standards

International

Article 25 of the International Covenant on Civil and Political Rights (ICCPR) guarantees the right of citizens to participate in public affairs and to vote and run for public office in free elections. The UN Human Rights Committee (HRC), the body of independent experts who review state compliance with the ICCPR, has determined that this article protects the right to "join organizations and associations concerned with political and public affairs," and that "political parties and membership in parties play a significant role in the conduct of public affairs...."[210]

---

[209] Ministry of Justice decisions permitting a new society to register are published in the *Official Gazette*. The pro-government political groups are: Al Asalah Islamic Society, Islamic, National Al Minbar Islamic Society (Al Minbar), Islamic, Al Shura Islamic Society, Islamic, The National Unity Gathering Society, Islamic, Al Saff Islamic Society, Islamic, Al Adala National Movement Society, Salafi, Al Rabita Islamic Society, Islamic, Shia, The Justice and Development Society, Shia, The National Action Charter Society, Liberal, Al Wasat al Arabi Democratic Islamic Society, Pan-Arab, The National Constitutional Gathering Society, The National Liberal Thinking Society, The National Will and Change Society, The National Dialogue Society (Al Hiwar). The opposition politcal groups are: Al Wefaq Islamic Society, Islamic, The Unitary National Democratic Society, Pan-Arab, The Nationalist Democratic Society, Pan-Arab, Al Ekha National Society (Al Ekha), The Progressive Democratic Tribune (Taqadumi), Leftist, The National Democratic Action Society (Wa'ad), Liberal, Al Amal Islamic Society (a court has ordered dissolved but the case remains under appeal).

[210] Human Rights Committee, General Comment No. 25: The right to participate in public affairs, voting rights and the right of equal access to public service (Art. 25), July 12, 1996, http://www.unhchr.ch/tbs/doc.nsf/(Symbol)/d0b7f023e8d6d9898025651e004bc0eb?Opendocument (accessed July 31, 2012).

Bahraini Law

Article 27 of Bahrain's 2002 Constitution guarantees the freedom to form associations, "under the rules and conditions laid down by law," provided that their objectives are lawful, carried out by peaceful means, and do not infringe on "the fundamentals of the religion and public order."[211]

Between 2001 and 2005, political societies registered under the 1989 Law of Associations. This law, as noted earlier, prohibits "engaging in politics," but authorities waived enforcement of this provision for all political societies.[212]

In 2004, a group of members of parliament proposed a draft law of political societies. The opposition groups, most of which had boycotted the national assembly elections of 2002 after the king had decreed a new constitution without consulting them, demanded to be included in drafting the law. According to Jawad Fairooz, a former Al-Wefaq deputy, the government decided to launch its own draft political societies law before opposition candidates were elected to the Chamber of Deputies and would have a say in drafting the law:

> In 2005, authorities realized that the opposition groups were going to participate in the 2006 national elections, so they drafted and passed a number of laws that restrict the ability of political societies to operate, such as the law on political societies, the anti-terrorism law, and the amended law on public gatherings.[213]

Opposition political societies were critical of several provisions of the law, including the prohibition of receiving "foreign funds or training," setting the minimum membership age at 21, and granting the Ministry of Justice authority to reject applications for registration.[214] The National Assembly passed the draft law in July 2005 without any input from the

---

[211] Bahrain Constitution, art. 27.

[212] Human Rights Watch, phone conversation with Jawad Fairooz, August 12, 2012.

[213] Ibid.

[214] US State Department, Bureau of Democracy, Human Rights, and Labor, "Country Reports on Human Rights Practices – 2005: Bahrain," March 8, 2006, http://www.state.gov/j/drl/rls/hrrpt/2005/61686.htm (accessed October 9, 2012).

opposition societies. King Hamad signed the bill into law on July 23, 2005. On July 29, several thousand people demonstrated to protest the legislation.[215]

Eventually most opposition groups accepted the political societies' law. Matar Matar, a former Al-Wefaq deputy, explained his society's decision:

> There was concern that boycotting the law would create tension between the government and the societies, and worse the government might use [a boycott] as a justification to crackdown on the societies. For this reason we decided to accept the law.[216]

Some opposition leaders though defied authorities by establishing political societies without seeking registration. For instance, Hassan Mushaima and Abduljalil al-Singace split from Al-Wefaq and established the Haq Movement for Liberty and Democracy (Haq) to protest Al-Wefaq's decision to abide by the new law and more generally to operate within the confines of the constitution decreed by the king in 2002.[217]

Under the law, a political society must have at least 50 co-founders in order to register. The Ministry of Justice can deny registration by informing the applicants and providing an explanation or by letting the 60-day deadline pass without a response.[218]

According to the law, political societies cannot be based on class, sect, geography, profession, religion, language, race, or sex.[219] This limitation on the themes and interests on which a political group may be based is too sweeping, especially given a government's duties to uphold equality and minority rights under article 27 of the ICCPR.[220]

---

[215] "Rally of group 8 demands (authorities) to drop or amend law of association, (مسيرة "الثماني" تطالب بإسقاط قانون الجمعيات أو تعديله)," *Al-Wasat*, July 30, 2005, http://www.alwasatnews.com/1058/news/read/480825/1.html (accessed November 15, 2011).

[216] Human Rights Watch, Skype interview with Matar Matar, August 8, 2012.

[217] "Al-Wefaq: Its Birth and Origins," Dr. Raed al-Jowdar, translated by Latifa, September 9, 2011, http://www.bahrainviews.com/?p=1420 (accessed October 23, 2012).

[218] Law No. 26/2005, art. 9.

[219] Ibid., art 4 (4). The article also prohibits the formation of political parties on the bases of "discrimination on the bases or sex, origin, language, religion or faith".

[220] Article 27 of the ICCPR states "In those States in which ethnic, religious or linguistic minorities exist, persons belonging to such minorities shall not be denied the right, in community with the other members of their group, to enjoy their own culture, to profess and practise their own religion, or to use their own language." International Covenant on Civil and Political Rights (ICCPR), adopted December 16, 1966, G.A., art. 27.

In effect, this provision gives authorities grounds to stop citizens from forming a political group that draws its main inspiration from, for example, religion, the advancement of women's interests, or particular regional interests. Any law on political parties should be drawn so as to allow the state to prohibit political groups only on the grounds that they advocate violence or the overthrow of democracy.[221]

The government provides financial allowances to officially registered political societies. However, several opposition groups told Human Rights Watch that the government halted their financial allowances before as well as after the pro-democracy demonstrations in February and March 2011.[222]

Human Rights Watch is not aware of any case where authorities denied registration to a political society seeking to register since the law took effect in 2005. Seven opposition societies—Al-Wefaq National Islamic Society, the National Democratic Assembly Society (al-Qawmi), the National Democratic Action Society (Wa'ad), the Unity Democratic Gathering Society (al-Wahdawi), the National Brotherhood Society (al-Akha), the Democratic Progressive Tribune (al-Taqadumi), and the Islamic Action Society (Amal, dissolved in 2012)—were able to register as of May 2013, although society leaders told Human Rights Watch that the process took several months.

The minister of justice can seek a court order to shut down a political society for up to three months if the latter "violates provisions of the constitution, the [political societies] law, or any other law."[223] The court must rule within 30 days, during which time the society is suspended. [224] The minister can also seek a court ruling to dissolve a political society if

---

[221] Human Rights Watch, *Tunisia's Repressive Laws: The Reform Agenda*, December 11, 2011, http://www.hrw.org/reports/2011/12/16/tunisia-s-repressive-laws-0.

[222] Wa'ad officials told Human Rights Watch that the group received 1,000 Bahraini Dinars (US$ 2,640) per month but the government halted the stipend in April 2011. Amal had been receiving 1,000 Bahraini Dinars per-month but the Ministry of Justice halted the allowance in October 2010. Other opposition groups also told Human Rights Watch that in the wake of the pro-democracy demonstrations in February 2011 the government has halted provision of stipends. Human Right Watch contacted opposition groups about the financial allowance s they receive from the government. On May 21, 2013, the Minister of Justice said at a parliamentary session that his ministry had "halted the financial allowances of some societies because they deviated from the purposes they were established for" without naming those political societies. See: "Minister of Justice: We paid 1,5 million dinars allowance to [political] societies until December 2012, (وزير العدل: دفعنا 1.5 مليون دينار لتمويل الجمعيات حتى ديسمبر 2012)," *Al-Wasat*, May 22, 2013, http://www.alwasatnews.com/3910/news/read/774280/1.html (accessed June 3, 2013).

[223] Law No. 26/2005, art. 22.

[224] Ibid.

the violation is "serious," a term the law does not define.[225] Under these provisions, authorities can seek the dissolution of any political society at any time, as they did with the Islamic Action Society (Amal) in June 2012. Persons who violate any provision of the law face up to three months imprisonment or fines of up to Bahraini Dinars 500 ($1,320).[226]

The law prohibits political groups from using public buildings such as schools and religious places for their activities, or from contacting political groups outside Bahrain without prior approval.[227] Political parties may not accept "donations" or "benefit" from a foreign person or entity.

Opposition groups say the law's vague language and intense governmental scrutiny impede their ability to operate. According to Jawad Fairooz, a former Al-Wefaq deputy:

> Authorities can interpret the provisions the way they like. Now they can say this conversation that I'm having with [Human Rights Watch] has benefited me because [this foreign organization] reports on my issues. So they can say that my group has violated the law.[228]

Opposition groups allege that authorities enforce the law in a discriminatory manner. One opposition leader who asked not to be named out of concern for his security said that while authorities strictly monitor every move of the opposition, they turn a blind eye to activities of pro-government groups. "They play double standards," this person said. "They have denied us permits for demonstrations claiming that we used places of worship, but it's completely fine for pro-government groups," referring to demonstrations in al-Fatih mosque in 2011. [229]

---

[225] Law No. 26/2005, art. 23.

[226] Ibid., art. 25.

[227] Ibid., art. 6 (4-f).

[228] Human Rights Watch, phone conversation with Jawad Fairooz, a former Al-Wefaq deputy, August 12, 2012. Human Right Watch also documented that some of those arrested in late 2010 were questioned about communications with HRW. See Human Rights Watch, *No Justice in Bahrain: Unfair Trials in Military and Civilian Courts*, February 28, 2012, http://www.hrw.org/reports/2012/02/28/no-justice-bahrain-0.

[229] Human Rights Watch Skype interview with an opposition leader (name withheld), August 9, 2012. Also see: "More than 100,000 citizens renew pledge of allegiance and loyalty to His Majesty the King and the wise leadership, (اكثر من 100 الف مواطن يجددون البيعة والولاء لجلالة الملك المفدى وقيادته الحكيمة)," *Bahrain News Agency*, February, 18, 2011, http://www.bna.bh/portal/news/447580?date=2011-02-22 (accessed August 13, 2012).

Restrictions on Political Societies

In August 2010, two months before scheduled national and municipal elections, authorities arrested scores of leaders and activists affiliated with unregistered parties and shut down websites and suspended newsletters of registered political societies.[230]

By September 2010, security forces had arrested dozens, including 25 opposition activists, whom they charged with plotting to topple the government, a violation of Bahrain's 2006 counterterrorism law. A Human Rights Watch investigation found that most of the charges, including "spreading false information" and "inciting hatred of the government," were related to their political views and writings.[231]

Restrictions on Peaceful Assembly

On February 14, 2011, tens of thousands of Bahrainis took part in street demonstrations throughout much of the country demanding greater political rights and government reform. Security forces used lethal force to suppress and disperse demonstrators. In mid-March King Hamad declared a three-month state of emergency under which security forces launched a campaign of retribution and arrested thousands who participated in or appeared to support the protests, including leaders of registered political societies. Authorities also again blocked websites of political societies.

On April 7, 2011, authorities shut down for several months the National Democratic Action Society (Wa'ad), a registered political group representing secular and leftist critics of the government.[232]

Among those arrested were Wa'ad leader Ibrahim Sharif and Shaikh Muhammad Ali al-Mahfoodh, leader of the Islamic Action Society (Amal). On June 22, 2011, a special military

---

[230] "Bahrain: Elections to Take Place Amid Crackdown," Human Rights Watch news release, October 20, 2010, http://www.hrw.org/news/2010/10/20/bahrain-elections-take-place-amid-crackdown. The opposition activists were released in February 2011 amid popular pro-democracy demonstrations. See "Bahrain: Ensure Rights of Freed Political Prisoners," Human Rights Watch news release, February 25, 2011, http://www.hrw.org/news/2011/02/24/bahrain-ensure-rights-freed-political-prisoners.

[231] "Bahrain: Elections to Take Place Amid Crackdown," Human Rights Watch, news release, October 20, 2010, http://www.hrw.org/news/2010/10/20/bahrain-elections-take-place-amid-crackdown.

[232] The National Democratic Action Society (Wa'ad) was permitted to re-open in late June 2011. "The National Democratic Action Society Suspended, (ايقاف جمعية العمل الوطني)," Bahrain News Agency, April 7, 2011, http://www.bna.bh/portal/news/452058?date=2011-04-15 (accessed December 3, 2012).

court convicted Sharif and 20 others and sentenced them to long prison terms. Sharif was sentenced to five years. In October 2011, a military court sentenced Shaikh al-Mahfoodh to 10 years imprisonment, reduced on appeal to five years.

Human Rights Watch examined trial verdicts and other court documents in those cases and concluded that these defendants were charged and convicted solely of offenses related to speeches they made, meetings they attended, documents found on their computers, and calls they made for peaceful street protests.[233]

The Bahrain Independent Commission of Inquiry (BICI), which King Hamad bin Isa Al Khalifa appointed to investigate the government's response to pro-democracy demonstrations in February and March 2011, concluded that many detainees—including opposition society leaders and activists—were subjected to torture and coerced into signing confessions, which were used to secure their convictions. The report said "there was a more discernible pattern of mistreatment with regard to … the 14 political leaders," adding that the ill-treatment was "to obtain statements or confessions incriminating [themselves]" or for "retribution and punishment."[234] A High Court of Appeal, and later the Court of Cassation, upheld the convictions and sentences against all the political leaders.[235]

Restrictions on the right of legally recognized political societies to exercise the right to peaceful assembly continued in the aftermath of the political turmoil of 2011.

On June 19, 2012, Al-Wefaq leaders requested permission to hold a gathering on June 22 in the al-Bilad al-Qadeem area in Manama. A day before the planned demonstration, the Ministry of Interior denied the request, claiming that it would "disrupt public security and harm the interests of people." Jawad Fairooz told Human Rights Watch that authorities had previously allowed them to demonstrate in the same area, but that the ministry had rejected four gathering requests from Al-Wefaq that week. "This seems to be a trend towards imposing more restrictions of freedom," he said.

---

233 Human Rights Watch, *No Justice in Bahrain: Unfair Trials in Military and Civilian Courts*, February 28, 2012, http://www.hrw.org/reports/2012/02/28/no-justice-bahrain-0.

234 Report of the Independent Commission of Inquiry, November 23, 2011, http://www.bici.org.bh/BICIreportEN.pdf, para. 1230, (accessed October 23, 2012).

235 "Bahrain: Highest Court Upholds Grossly Unfair Convictions," Human Rights Watch news release, January 7, 2013, http://www.hrw.org/news/2013/01/07/bahrain-highest-court-upholds-grossly-unfair-convictions.

A ministry statement on June 21 said it had permitted Al-Wefaq to hold "27 rallies [and 20 gatherings] since the beginning of 2012," suggesting there should be a limit on the number of demonstrations per year. [236]

Hani al-Shaikh, a member of the National Democratic Action Society political bureau, confirmed that in June 2012 authorities revived the policy of routinely denying permission for political rallies, saying:

> Authorities increasingly prevent opposition societies from holding rallies and gatherings. They used to deny permit for areas they consider "vital for the public life" which included some streets. However, they have gradually expanded this definition to include many areas of the capital as well as surrounding villages. [237]

On May 7, 2013, the Chamber of Deputies passed an amendment to the Public Gathering Law to severely limit the right to peaceful public assembly. Under the new amendments, demonstration organizers would have to deposit a security check of up to 20,000 Bahraini Dinars (US$53,000) in order to hold a public gathering and authorities can reject protest permissions for vague terms including demonstrations that might " threaten or restrict the freedom of others... and might harm the economic interests if the country." The new amendments would ban demonstrations near "hospitals, airports, embassies, consulates, economic, and lively places, and places that has security nature." [238] The new amendment needs approval from the Shura Council and King Hamad's signature to become law.

The ICCPR makes clear that restrictions on peaceful demonstrations should be imposed only if found to be "necessary in a democratic society" to safeguard "national security or public safety, public order (*ordre public*), the protection of public health or morals or the protection of the rights and freedoms of others." Any restrictions must also be proportional and non-discriminatory. [239]

---

[236] "Chief of Public Security: Decided to prevent the rally called for by Al Wefaq..., (رئيس الأمن العام: تقرر منع المسيرة التي دعت إليها)
(الوفاق)," Ministry of Interior, June 21, 2012, http://www.policemc.gov.bh/news_details.aspx?type=1&articleId=11791 (accessed June 27, 2012).

[237] Human Rights Watch, phone conversation with Hani al-Shaikh, August 10, 2012.

[238] Amendments to Public Gathering Law, arts. 2 (a), 4, 11. Copy on file with Human Rights Watch. The amendment was proposed by five members of the Chamber of Deputies in January 2013.

[239] International Covenant on Civil and Political Rights (ICCPR), adopted December 16, 1966, G.A., art. 21.

Restrictions on Freedom of Expression

Bahrain's Press Law (Law 47/2002) restricts coverage of topics that might, in the view of authorities, "harm the ruling system, its religion, and [disturb] public decency."[240] It also prescribes a minimum six months imprisonment for criticizing the king and up to five years for second-time offenders.[241] The law prohibits distributing any publication without receiving written approval from authorities, a provision that authorities have used to ban political societies from publishing in print and on the Internet.[242]

The Penal Code contains other articles that restrict the freedom of expression and information. For example, article 134 (A) sets a minimum of three months imprisonment and/or fines for anyone who fails to obtain government permission to attend meetings abroad to discuss Bahraini affairs that might "undermine financial confidence in the state" or who "exercises ... activities that are harmful to the national interests."[243] In November 2008, Interior Minister Rashid bin Abdullah Al Khalifa threatened to prosecute rights activists and opposition figures who had held meetings in Washington, DC.[244]

In September 2010, the Information Affairs Authority (IAA) blocked websites, newsletters, and blogs of at least three opposition political societies. On September 3, the IAA blocked the website of Al-Wefaq.[245] Abdullah Yateem, the general director of press and publications at the authority, said that Al-Wefaq had violated laws and regulations without specifying any provisions that the group had allegedly violated.[246] Al- Wefaq leaders believe that IAA's decision was related to the group's plan to launch an audiovisual service on its website in the run-up to elections.[247] Authorities only lifted these sanction on Al-Wefaq in November 2011, after the elections. Opposition newsletters of Al-Wefaq, the Islamic Action Society, and Wa'ad are still banned.

---

[240] Law No. 47/2002, art. 19.

[241] Ibid., art. 68.

[242] Ibid., art. 17.

[243] Law No. 15/1976, art., 134 (A).

[244] "Minister of Interior: Discussing internal issues abroad is a violation to the law, (وزير الداخلية: بحث الموضوعات الداخلية في الخارج مخالف للقانون)," Al-Wasat, November 6, 2008, http://www.alwasatnews.com/2253/news/read/22574/1.html (accessed November 10, 2011). In this instance authorities took no legal action against the individuals participating in those meetings.

[245] "IAA blocks Al-Wefaq website, (الإعلام تحجب الموقع الإلكتروني لـ الوفاق)," Al-Wasat, September 4, 2012, http://www.alwasatnews.com/2920/news/read/472942/1.html (accessed October 23, 2012).

[246] Ibid.

[247] Human Rights Watch, conversation with Jawad Fairooz, August 12, 2012.

In September 2010, municipal officials ordered Wa'ad Party candidate Munira Fakhro to remove billboards with the slogan "Enough to Corruption," saying it was "a breach of the law," although they did not indicate which law. A court ruled on October 4 that the signs did not violate any law, but the government appealed.[248] On October 14, 2010, the Third High Court of Appeal upheld the ruling.[249]

According to Fadhel Abbas, secretary general of the United National Democratic Assembly, a registered opposition political society, authorities were not happy with the content of his group's monthly newsletter, *Al-Badeel.* The issue published in July 2010 contained articles discussing alleged corruption in government institutions and sectarian discrimination.[250] Although authorities have not canceled *Al-Badeel*'s license, Abbas told Human Rights Watch in August 2012 he had no plan to resume publication. "We are sure they will ban it because they will not be happy with the content," he said.[251]

Since the suppression of street demonstrations beginning in March 2011, authorities have further restricted the right of political societies to freedom of expression. On April 7, 2011, the Bahrain Defense Force suspended the National Democratic Action Society, shut down its offices, and blocked its website "until further notice" after the group posted an article that the BDF charged was "defaming the armed forces and spreading false news that foment sedition and drives wedges among citizens."[252] The ban was lifted when Wa'ad agreed to participate in the government-sponsored National Dialogue in July 2011.[253]

During the 10-week state of emergency, from March 15 to June 1, 2011, several offices and homes of leaders of political societies were either attacked by unknown assailants or raided by security forces who broke doors, windows, and furniture and confiscated documents and computers.[254] At midnight on March 25, for a second time that month,

---

[248] Human Rights Watch, World Report 2011 (New York, Human Rights Watch), Bahrain chapter, http://www.hrw.org/world-report-2011/world-report-2011-bahrain.

[249] "Appeal upholds the slogan "Enough to Corruption, (الاستئناف تؤكد صحة رفع شعار: بسنا فساد)," *Al-Wasat*, October 15, 2010, http://www.alwasatnews.com/2961/news/read/488310/1.html (accessed, August 27, 2012).

[250] Al-Badeel, Unitary National Democratic Assembly, June-July 2010, http://www.tjm3.org/resources/pdf/B4.pdf (accessed August 10, 2012).

[251] Human Rights Watch, phone conversation with Fadhel Abbas, August 13, 2012.

[252] "National Democratic Action Society - Wa'ad – Suspended," *Bahrain News Agency*, April 7, 2011, http://bna.bh/portal/en/news/452065?date=2011-04-7 (accessed August 10).

[253] "Bahrain to Lift Ban on a Political Association," *Bahrain News Agency*, June 18, 2011, http://bna.bh/portal/en/news/461301 (accessed August 10, 2012).

[254] Human Rights Watch, phone conversation with members of various opposition groups, August 10, 11, and 12 2012.

unknown assailants attacked the house of Wa'ad leader Munira Fakhro in A'ali, south of Manama. She told a local newspaper:

> We heard the sound of two explosions. I and members of my family went to look for the source of the sound and we found that the [assailants] had broken the back door and the window of my house. They then had thrown the bombs which resulted in damages to the house. [255]

At the same time government media, including the state-run Bahrain News Agency, and pro-government groups launched a smear campaign labeling leaders of opposition political societies as "traitors" and "pro-Iran." A banner from of Al-Asala Islamic Group, a pro-government political society, read: "The diseased spots in the body of the nation must be eradicated."[256] The banner contained pictures of Wa'ad leader Ibrahim Sharif, as well as leaders of unlicensed opposition groups, including Hassan Mushaima, Abduljalil al-Singace, and Abd al-Wahab Hussein.

The BICI called on the government to relax "censorship and [allow] the opposition greater access to television broadcasts, radio broadcasts and print media."[257] In January 2012, Al-Wefaq submitted an application to launch a satellite TV channel in Bahrain.[258] Authorities had not responded to the request as of May 2013.[259] In November 2011, Al-Wefaq requested a license to publish a daily newspaper but the official response was not encouraging, "They said we needed to do many things, among them establishing a company with an investment of at least one million dinars ($2,639,000)," Jawad Fairooz said. "Frankly, we don't have the financial ability to shoulder it."[260]

---

[255] "Second attack on Munira Fakhro's home, (هجوم ثانٍ على منزل منيرة فخرو)," *Al-Wasat*, March 25, 2012, http://www.alwasatnews.com/3122/news/read/534040/1.html (accessed October 23, 2012).

[256] Picture of the banner is on file at Human Rights Watch.

[257] Report of the Independent Commission of Inquiry, November 23, 2011, http://www.bici.org.bh/BICIreportEN.pdf, para. 1724 (b), (accessed October 23, 2012).

[258] "Al-Wefaq requests a license to launch a satellite channel, (الوفاق تطلب الترخيص لإطلاق قناة فضائية)," *Al-Wasat*, January 4, 2012, http://www.alwasatnews.com/3406/news/read/619550/1.html (accessed January 10, 2012)

[259] Human Rights Watch, phone conversation with Jawad Fairooz, June 25, 2012.

[260] Ibid. Also see: "Al-Wefaq seeks publishing a daily newspaper, («الوفاق» تتقدم بطلب لإصدار صحيفة يومية)," *Al-Wasat*, December 4, 2011, http://www.alwasatnews.com/3375/news/read/612673/1.html (accessed May 7, 2013).

On November 6, 2012, the Ministry of Interior summarily revoked the citizenship of the 31 people, including Jawad Fairooz, leaving the majority of those affected stateless.[261]

On April 23, 2013 the Public Prosecution held Fadhel Abbas, secretary general of the United National Democratic Assembly, for 48 hours on charges of "inciting hatred against the regime" in a speech he gave at a press conference on April 20. The Public Prosecution released him on April 25.[262]

Article 19 of the ICCPR protects the "freedom to seek, receive and impart information and ideas of all kinds, regardless of frontiers, either orally, in writing or in print, in the form of art, or through any other media of his choice." Any restrictions on this right must be provided by law and strictly necessary to "respect the rights or reputations of others" or "for the protection of national security or of public order or public health and morals."[263]

The UN Human Rights Committee (HRC) determined that "all public figures, including those exercising the highest political authority such as heads of state and government, are legitimately subject to criticism and political opposition" and therefore the need for "uninhibited expression" in public debate concerning public figures is very high. It also says that "prohibitions of displays of lack of respect for a religion or other belief system, including blasphemy laws, are incompatible with the Covenant" except in very limited circumstances.[264]

---

[261] Other the political leaders and activists included Jalal Fairooz, a former member of parliament, Saeed al-Shihabi, Ali Hassan Mushaima,, Abdul-Raouf al-Shaib, Abdul-Hadi Khalaf, and Abbas Omran. See: "Revoking Citizenship of 31 Bahrainis Among Them Religious Clerics, Tow Former Members of Parliament and a Lawyer, (إسقاط الجنسية عن 31 بحرينيا بينهم رجال دين ونائبان سابقان ومحام)," *Al-Wasat*, November 7, 2012, http://www.alwasatnews.com/3714/news/read/714002/1.html (accessed April 1, 2013). "Bahrain: Don't Arbitrarily Revoke Citizenship," Human Rights Watch press release, November 8, 2012, http://www.hrw.org/news/2012/11/08/bahrain-don-t-arbitrarily-revoke-citizenship.

[262] "The Public Prosecution Office releases Fadhel Abbas and subjects him to a travel ban, (النيابة تخلي سبيل فاضل عباس بضمان محل إقامته)," *Al-Wasat*, April 25, 2013, http://www.alwasatnews.com/3883/news/read/767166/1.html (accessed May 7, 2013). He told Human Rights Watch as of June 5, 2013 that he does not know whether the Public Prosecution Officer has referred his case to the criminal court. Human Rights Watch, phone conversation with Fadhel Abbas, secretary general of the United National Democratic Assembly, June 5, 2013.

[263] International Covenant on Civil and Political Rights (ICCPR), adopted December 16, 1966, G.A.Res. 2200A (XXI), 21 UN GAOR Supp. (No. 16) at 52, UN Doc. A/6316 (1966), 999 UNT.S.

[264] Human Rights Committee, General Comment No. 10: Freedom of expression (Art. 19), June 29, 1983, http://www.unhchr.ch/tbs/doc.nsf/(Symbol)/2bb2f14bf558182ac12563ed0048df17?Opendocument (accessed August 7, 2012).

National Dialogue of 2011

In July 2011, in the aftermath of the suppression of pro-democracy protests, the government sponsored what it called a National Dialogue which it said aimed at presenting "the people's views and demands for further reform."[265]

Al-Wefaq and the National Democratic Action Society participated but complained about insufficient representation: all opposition groups combined were given only 35 seats out of more than 300 seats.[266]

The national dialogue recommendations submitted to the government included further restrictions on the activities of political societies, such as prohibiting "any activity that might harm the economy and public interest," "using religion for political gains," and "discussing sectarian issues."[267] The government commission assigned to implement the recommendations of the National Dialogue reported that the government has drafted an amendment to the political societies law, but at time of writing the government had not submitted the amendment to the National Assembly.[268]

Disbanding the Islamic Action Society (Amal)

The Islamic Action Society (Amal) was founded in 2002 under the provisions of the Law of Associations. Authorities renewed the society's license after the Law of Political Societies took effect in 2005. Prior to the widespread suppression of opposition activities in 2011, Amal had about 2,000 members. It traces its roots to the Islamic Front for the Liberation of Bahrain, which had been accused of planning a coup to topple the government in 1981.[269]

---

[265] "About the National Dialogue", National Dialogue, http://www.nd.bh/en/index.php/the-dialogue/about (accessed August 10, 2012).

[266] Aurore Cloe Dupuis "Bahrain's main opposition group to quit national dialogue," France 24, July 17, 2011, http://www.france24.com/en/20110717-bahrain-main-opposition-shiite-group-quit-national-dialogue-reform (accessed August 10, 2012). In February 2013 the opposition groups, pro-government groups and the Bahraini government launched a new round of negotiations aimed at addressing the political crisis. After many rounds of talks the pro-government groups and the government have yet to agree to some opposition demands including having a representative of the royal family participate in the negotiations and conducting a popular referendum to ratify the outcome.

[267] "Report of Government Committee assigned to implement visions of the National Dialogue, (تقرير اللجنة المكلفة بتنفيذ مرئيات حوار التوافق الوطني)," http://www.nd.bh/ar/index.php/the-dialogue/final-report#pc (accessed August 10, 2012).

[268] "The government completed a draft amendment to political societies' law, (الحكومة الموقرة أكملت مشروع تعديل قانون الجمعيات السياسية)," http://www.nd.bh/ar/index.php/implementation/committee-news/item/150 (accessed August 10, 2012).

[269] "Religious body floats demands for elections," Gulf News, March 6, 2008, http://gulfnews.com/news/gulf/bahrain/religious-body-floats-demands-for-elections-1.227902 (accessed October 23, 2012).

Among the society's stated objectives are the establishment of a "pluralist political system … and protecting its Arab and Islamic identity."[270]

In May 2005, authorities closed Amal's offices for 45 days after it had organized a ceremony honoring 73 individuals who had been prosecuted for allegedly planning a coup in 1981.[271]

On December 19, 2007, security forces raided Amal's offices, claiming they were suspicious that weapons were hidden there. No weapons were found.[272] A few weeks earlier, authorities had arrested two members and charged them with stealing police weapons; they were subsequently acquitted.[273]

In May 2008, the Ministry of Justice canceled the society's general assembly, saying the group violated the law by holding the event in Ma'tam al-Huda, in the village of al-Sar, which the ministry considered a place of worship, and stopped the state's BD 1,000 (US $2,640) monthly financial allowance.[274]

As part of government's ban on publications of opposition groups ahead of the October 2010 Chamber of Deputies elections, on September 30 authorities canceled the license of the society's newsletter and blocked its website.[275] In December 2010, the Ministry of Justice froze Amal's bank accounts without notice or explanation. [276]

Following the February and March 2011 demonstrations, security forces arrested dozens of Amal members, including 23 high ranking members.[277] On April 14, 2011, the Ministry of Justice announced that it would seek a court order to dissolve Al-Wefaq and Amal,

---

[270] "The Islamic Action Society, Who we are?, (الجبهة العمل الاسلامي، من نحن؟)," The Islamic Action Society, http://www.amal-islami.net/index.php?plugin=pages&act=read_page&id=1 (accessed, August 27,2012).

[271] Human Rights Watch, phone conversation with Hisham al-Sabagh, a leader Amal political society, August 12, 2012.

[272] Ibid.

[273] Ibid.

[274] Ma'atms are sites for social and religious gatherings for Shias. "MOJ leans towards cancelling the election results of the Islamic Action Society, (العدل تتجه لإلغاء نتيجة انتخابات جمعية العمل الإسلام)," Al-Ayam, May, 17, 2008, http://www.amal-islami.net/index.php?plugin=news&act=news_read&id=1168 (accessed October 24, 2012).

[275] In October 2010 the Ministry of Justice halted the monthly allowance. Human Rights Watch, email correspondence with Hajar al-Mahfoodh, April 9, 2013.

[276] Human Rights Watch, interview with Hajar al-Mahfoodh, daughter of Muhammad al-Mahfoodh, Manama, December 3, 2011.

[277] Ibid.

accusing both groups of violating "the Constitution and being involved in acts that damaged the public peace and national unity…"[278] The next day authorities dropped the case after the United States publicly urged the government to reverse its decision.[279]

Authorities tried 23 Amal members before a special military court on charges that included "inciting hatred against the regime," "broadcasting false and tendentious news and rumors," and "calling for protests."[280] On October 4, 2011, the military court sentenced Shaikh al-Mahfoodh and four others to 10 years imprisonment and nine others to 5 years imprisonment. The rest were acquitted.[281] The High Court of Appeal confirmed the convictions but reduced the sentence of Shaikh al-Mahfoodh and three others from ten years to five years.[282]

On June 3, 2012, the Ministry of Justice sought a court order to dissolve Amal, accusing the groups of "flagrant and continuous violations," such as failing to "convene a general conference for more than four years," "taking its decisions from a religious authority that calls openly for violence and incites hatred," and "failing to submit a copy of its annual budget as per the [political societies] law's provisions."[283]

On June 19, the Administrative Court held the first session on the ministry's complaint; the judge adjourned the hearing to October 7, but without prior notice subsequently moved up the date of the hearing and on July 9 ordered the dissolution of Amal for violating provisions of the Political Societies' law.[284] On April 15, 2013, the Court of Appeal upheld the ruling.[285]

---

[278] "Ministry of Justice: lawsuit to dissolve Amal and Al-Wefaq, (العدل": دعاوى قضائية لحل جمعيتي "الوفاق" و"العمل الإسلامي"))," *Al-Wasat*, April 14, 2011, http://www.alwasatnews.com/3141/news/read/537258/1.html (accessed August 10, 2012).

[279] "Bahrain says will not disband opposition groups: minister," Reuters, April 15, 2011, http://www.reuters.com/article/2011/04/15/us-bahrain-idUSTRE73E3J520110415 (accessed August 11, 2012).

[280] Human Rights Watch, conversation with Hajar al-Mahfoodh, Manama, December 3, 2011.

[281] Human Rights Watch, phone conversation with Hisham al-Sabagh, August 12, 2012.

[282] The court also reduced the sentences of three Amal members from five years to one year; reduced the sentences of two members from five year to six months and one month respectively; and acquitted another one. See: "Court reduces the punishment of Amal members, (المحكمة تُخفض عقوبة كوادر أمل))," *al-Wasat*, November 29, 2012, http://www.alwasatnews.com/3736/news/read/719353/1.html (accessed, December 3, 2012).

[283] "Justice Ministry Files Case against Amal," Bahrain News Agency, June 3, 2012, http://bna.bh/portal/en/news/511420?date=2012-06-3 (Accessed June 25, 2012).

[284] "Bahrain: the court issues judgment to dissolve the Islamic Action Society, (البحرين: القضاء يصدر حكما بحل جمعية العمل الإسلامي))," Al-Sharq Al-Awsat, July, 10, 2012, http://www.aawsat.com/details.asp?article=685722 (accessed October 24, 2012).

[285] "The Court of Appeal uphold the dissolution of Amal, («الاستئناف» تؤيد حل جمعية «أمل»))," *Al-Wasat*, April 16, 2013, http://www.alwasatnews.com/3874/news/read/764593/1.html (accessed May 7, 2013).

On April 26, 2013, security forces raided the Sanabis home of an Amal leader, Hisham al-Sabagh, and arrested him. His brother Nadir al-Sabagh told *Al-Wasat* newspaper that authorities allowed his family to see Hisham only after 12 days in detention. At time of this writing, authorities had not allowed Sabagh's lawyers to see him and had not charged him with any crimes.[286]

---

[286] "Hisham al-Sanagh's family meet with him after 12 days of his arrest, (عائلة هشام الصباغ تلتقيه اليوم بعد اعتقاله منذ 12 يوماً)," *Al-Wasat*, May 7, 2013, http://www.alwasatnews.com/3895/news/read/770130/1.html# (accessed May 7, 2013).

IV. Trade Unions

Under Bahraini law private sector workers and employees can establish trade unions without prior official approval, simply by notifying authorities. Public sector trade unions are not permitted but public sector, workers can join private sector unions.

The Workers Trade Union Law (Law 33/2002) permits workers to form and join unions and established the General Federation of Bahrain Trade Unions (GFBTU).[287] Until late 2011, the GFBTU served as the sole umbrella organization for trade unions in Bahrain, and the law allowed only one trade union per company.

In October 2011, King Hamad issued a decree amending Law 33/2002 to allow the establishment of more than one trade union in a company and more than one trade union federation in Bahrain. The GFBTU understood this as permitting the establishment of an explicitly pro-government trade union federation in retribution for GFBTU's support for protesters' calls for greater political rights and calling general strikes in February and March 2011. After the amendment became effective in March 2012, pro-government unionists established the Bahrain Free Labour Unions Federation. The new federation has accused the GFBTU of being a political tool of the opposition groups, saying that it "distorts Bahrain's reputation regionally and internationally."[288]

Private and public sector firms fired approximately 4,500 employees after the declaration of emergency law in March 2011.[289] By November 2012, most workers had been reinstated, although in many cases not to the positions and jobs from which they had been dismissed.[290] According to the GFBTU, more than 300 were still waiting to be reinstated.[291]

---

[287] Law 33/2002, art.1.

[288] "Al-Binali calls for halting government's assistance for the GFBTU, (البنعلي يدعو لإيقاف الدعم الحكومي عن اتحاد العمال), *Al-Watan*, August 29, 2012, http://www.alwatannews.net/NewsViewer.aspx?ID=Z_838_PJ_737_NHBVXJ9iLf4TWSRkg_939__939_&item=x (accessed May 29, 2013)

[289] Report of the Independent Commission of Inquiry, November 23, 2011, http://www.bici.org.bh/BICIreportEN.pdf, para. 1659, (accessed October 23, 2012).

[290] Bahrain: Promises Unkept, Rights Still Violated, press release, November 22, 2012, http://www.hrw.org/news/2012/11/22/bahrain-promises-unkept-rights-still-violated

[291] Human Rights Watch email correspondence with General Federation of Bahrain Trade Unions provided the figure to Human Rights Watch, June 10, 2013

Legal Standards

International

Article 22 of the International Covenant on Civil and Political Rights (ICCPR) guarantees individuals "the right to freedom of association with others."[292] Bahrain. a member of the International Labour Organization (ILO), has ratified four core ILO conventions, including both conventions relating to elimination of forced and compulsory labor, and those on the elimination of discrimination in respect of employment and occupation, but not Convention 87 on Freedom of Association and Protection of the Right to Organise or Convention 98 on the Right to Organise and Collective Bargaining.[293]

Article 2 of the ILO's Convention 87 states that "workers and employers, without distinction whatsoever, shall have the right to establish and, subject only to the rules of the organization concerned, to join organizations of their own choosing without previous authorization." The ILO requires governments to refrain from punishing workers for trying to organize unions and enforce mechanisms that deter employers from taking action against union organizers.

Bahraini Law

Article 27 of the Bahraini Constitution states that the right to form trade unions for "lawful objectives and by peaceful means is guaranteed under the rules and conditions laid down by law, provided that the fundamentals of the religion and public order are not infringed."[294] Article 10 of Law 33/2002 states that workers of "any particular establishment or sector ... can form their own trade union."[295] The law requires only that those wishing to establish a trade union should provide the Ministry of Labor with names of the founding members and bylaws of the union.[296]

---

[292] International Covenant on Civil and Political Rights (ICCPR), adopted December 16, 1966, G.A. Res. 2200A (XXI), 21 UN GAOR Supp. (No. 16) at 52, UN Doc. A/6316 (1966), 999 UNT.S. 171, entered into force March 23, 1976. Bahrain ratified the ICCPR in 2006.

[293] International Labour Organization, Decent Work Pilot Programme, Country Brief: Bahrain, http://www.ilo.org/public/english/bureau/dwpp/download/bahrain/countrybriefbah.pdf (accesses June 25, 2012).

[294] Bahrain Constitution, art. 27.

[295] Law 33/2002, art. 10. Amended by Decree No. 49 of 2006, Decree No. 35 of 2011.

[296] Ibid.

Restrictions on Trade Unions

Freedom to Form and Join Unions

Immediately after the law came into effect authorities denied public sector workers the right to establish or join unions, insisting that article 10 of the law does not cover them, although authorities later said that public sector workers can join private sector unions.[297]

In September 2004, the GFBTU and a dozen trade unions filed a lawsuit challenging the Civil Service Bureau's interpretation of the law. In February 2005, an administrative court dismissed the case, saying it fell outside of its jurisdiction. The Court of Appeal agreed.[298]

In June and October 2005, the GFBTU filed two complaints with the ILO protesting the government's repeated refusal to register six trade unions in the public sector. [299] Those were the Post Office Workers, Water and Electricity Workers, Public Works Workers, Healthcare Workers, Social Insurance Workers, and Retirement Fund Workers.[300]

In response to an ILO inquiry, the government said in 2006 that an amendment to the law to grant public workers the right to form trade unions was before the Chamber of Deputies.[301] In February 2013, Ministry of Labor officials told Human Rights Watch that the draft amendment was still before the Chamber of Deputies.[302] GFBTU leaders said they were not aware of such a draft amendment.[303]

In March 2007, the Civil Service Bureau threatened to take disciplinary actions against any workers in the public sector who attempt to establish trade unions, reiterating that public

---

[297] Civil Service Bureau, directive No. 3 of 2007, https://www.csb.gov.bh/csb/wcms/ar/home/laws-regulations/csb_legislation_in_effect/csb-governance/atta/G-003-2007.pdf (accessed August 6, 2012).

[298] International Federation for Human Rights and Arab Institute for Human Rights. "Freedom of Association in the Arabian Gulf: The case of Bahrain, Kuwait, and Yemen," http://www.fidh.org/IMG/pdf/etude.pdf (accessed August 6, 2012).

[299] International Labor Organization, Committee on Freedom of Association, Complaint against the Government of Bahrain presented by the General Federation of Bahrain Trade Union (GFBTU) Report No. 340, Case No. 2552 (2006). paras. 309-372. http://www.ilo.org/public/english/standards/relm/gb/docs/gb295/pdf/gb-8-1.pdf (accessed July 15, 2012).

[300] The list was provided by the GFBTU in November 2012. These unregistered unions still exist.

[301] International Labour Organization, Committee on Freedom of Association, Complaint against the Government of Bahrain presented by the General Federation of Bahrain Trade Union (GFBTU) Report No. 340, Case No. 2552 (2006). paras. 309-327. http://www.ilo.org/public/english/standards/relm/gb/docs/gb295/pdf/gb-8-1.pdf (accessed July 15, 2012).

[302] Human Rights Watch conversation with Abbas Matooq, Chief for International Relations and Ahmed Alhaiki, Director of Inspection for Labor Unions, Ministry of Labor, Manama, February 26, 2013.

[303] Human Rights Watch interview with Salman al-Mahfoodh, secretary general of the GFBTU, Manama, February 28, 2013.

sector workers do not have the right to establish their own trade unions but can join unions in the private sector.[304]

Restrictions on the Right to Strike

Law 33/2002 bans unions from "engaging in political activities" and imposes numerous restrictions on the right to strike. According to article 21, trade union members can strike only if 75 percent of the general assembly of the particular union approves the action and after they fail to resolve issues with their employer. Before going on strike they must give two weeks' notice to the employer and also notify the Ministry of Labor.

The law bans strikes in "vital and important facilities" such as "security, civil defense, airports, ports, hospitals, transportations, telecommunications, electricity, and water facilities."[305] In November 2006, the prime minister issued an edict prohibiting strikes in additional sectors on the grounds that strikes in those facilities would "endanger national security and disrupt daily life of people." The added facilities included "bakeries, all means of transporting people and goods, educational establishments and oil and gas installations."[306]

In 2007, the GFBTU filed complaints with the ILO protesting the prime minister's edict. The government responded that the ILO's Committee on Freedom of Association allows governments to regulate and prohibit strikes, saying it exercised its authority to ban strikes in facilities deemed essentials and that their interruption "would lead to the disruption of everyday life."[307]

In 2008, the ILO's Committee on Freedom of Association called on the government to amend its trade union law and the prime minister's ruling by providing a more limited definition of "essential services." The existing list was "broader than the definition of

---

[304] Civil Service Bureau, directive No. 3 of 2007, https://www.csb.gov.bh/csb/wcms/ar/home/laws-regulations/csb_legislation_in_effect/csb-governance/atta/G-003-2007.pdf (accessed August 6, 2012).

[305] Law 33 of 2002, art. 21.

[306] "Resolution No. 62 of 2006 in regard to specifying vital facilities in which strikes are prohibited, (قرار رقم (62) لسنة 2006)، (بشأن تحديد المنشآت الحيوية المحظور بها الإضراب)," Legal and Legislation Affairs Commission, http://www.legalaffairs.gov.bh/viewhtm.aspx?ID=RCAB6206 (accessed August 4, 2012)

[307] International Labour Organization, Committee on Freedom of Association, Complaint against the Government of Bahrain presented by the General Federation of Bahrain Trade Union (GFBTU) Report No. 349, Case No. 2552 (2008), paras. 408-424. http://www.ilo.org/wcmsp5/groups/public/@ed_norm/@relconf/documents/meetingdocument/wcms_091464.pdf (accessed July 15, 2012).

essential services in the strict sense of the term," the committee concluded. [308] The committee said that the government can only ban strikes in essential services -- "that is, services the interruption of which would endanger the life, personal safety, or health of the whole or part of the population." The committee further said that in order to prohibit a strike authorities need to establish "the existence of a clear and imminent threat to the life, personal safety, or health of the whole or part of the population."[309] As of February 2013 the government had not responded to the ILO communication.

Retribution after the 2011 Demonstrations

In the wake of the government's suppression of demonstrations in March 2011, the federation called for a general strike on March 13, claiming the situation on the streets made it too dangerous for employees to go to their jobs. Private and public sector businesses subsequently dismissed thousands of workers suspected of participating in or otherwise supporting the demonstrations. Employers frequently claimed that they fired workers because they did not show up for work.

A Human Rights Watch investigation in July 2011 found that private and public sector companies had violated Bahraini labor laws as well as international standards, "in particular those prohibiting discrimination on the basis of political opinion."[310] The summary dismissals of workers appeared to be "punishment for having participated in or otherwise supported pro-democracy demonstrations."[311]

The BICI investigation reported that according to government officials, 2,462 private sector and 1,945 public sector employees were fired following the March 2011 clampdown on protesters and concluded that many workers were fired despite being absent for periods that were shorter than "the periods proscribed as punishable" by the law.[312] The commission also concluded that in some sectors dismissals were "motivated by retaliation against employees suspected of being involved in the demonstrations."[313]

---

[308] Ibid.

[309] Ibid.

[310] "Bahrain: Revoke Summary Firings Linked to Protests," Human Rights Watch, news release, July 14, 2011, http://www.hrw.org/news/2011/07/14/bahrain-revoke-summary-firings-linked-protests.

[311] Ibid.

[312] Report of the Independent Commission of Inquiry, November 23, 2011, http://www.bici.org.bh/BICIreportEN.pdf, paras. 1659 and 1449, (accessed October 23, 2012).

[313] Ibid., para. 1450.

The BICI called on authorities to ensure that workers had not been dismissed because of the exercise of their right to freedom of expression, opinion, association or peaceful assembly.[314] In response to the government's claim that the strikes called for by the GFBTU were unlawful because they were not related to labor issues, the commission said it appeared those strikes "occurred…within the permissible bounds of the law."[315]

In August 2011, King Hamad ordered the reinstatement of dismissed employees.[316] Many private and public sector employers did not comply with the call. In November 2011, the government agreed to form a tripartite labor committee (comprising representatives of the ILO, the GFBTU, and the Ministry of Labor) under the auspice of ILO to address the issues. Under the terms of the agreement announced on March 11, 2012, all workers in the public and private sectors would be reinstated by no later than May 30, 2012.[317]

On December 31, 2011, the government announced that it would reinstate all public sector employees who had been dismissed for exercising their right to freedom of expression. The same announcement also said that authorities "negotiated with the private companies" and that the cases of dismissed workers would be resolved "soon."[318] However, as of June 10 2013 the GFBTU estimated that more than 300 employees in both the public and private sectors have not been reinstated in their jobs.[319]

In April 2011, the American Federation of Labor and Congress of Industrial Organizations (AFL/CIO) filed a complaint with the US Department of Labor alleging that Bahrain had violated provisions of the US-Bahrain Free Trade Agreement. The US Labor Department December 2012 report found that Bahrain had "acted inconsistently with its commitments

---

[314] Ibid., para 1456.

[315] Ibid., para. 1448.

[316] "Speech of the king on the occasion of the last ten days of the holy month of Ramadan, (كلمة عاهل البلاد بمناسبة العشر الأواخر من شهر رمضان المبارك)," *Al-Wasat*, August 28, 2011, http://www.alwasatnews.com/3277/news/read/591868/1.html (accessed August 27, 2012).

[317] International Labor Organization, Committee on Freedom of Association, Complaint against the Government of Bahrain presented by the International Trade Union Confederation (ITUC), Report No. 364, Case No. 2882 (2012). paras. 232-308. http://www.ilo.org/wcmsp5/groups/public/---ed_norm/---relconf/documents/meetingdocument/wcms_183430.pdf (accessed July 15, 2012).

[318] "Government renews its commitment to implement the recommendations of the (BICI) and discloses the steps, (الحكومة تجدد التزامها بتنفيذ توصيات تقصي الحقائق وتكشف خطواتها)," Bahrain News Agency, December 31, 2011, http://bna.bh/portal/news/487260?date=2012-01-1 (accessed August 10, 2012).

[319] Human Rights Watch email correspondence with General Federation of Bahrain Trade Unions provided the figure to Human Rights Watch, June 10, 2013

to … ensure that its laws recognize and protect freedom of association and the elimination of employment discrimination [and are] consistent with internationally recognized labor rights."[320] In May 2013, the US government requested talks with the Bahraini government to discuss the steps Bahrain has taken to address the issues raised in the Labor Department report.[321]

The 2011 Amendment Affecting Trade Union Rights

On October 9, 2011, King Hamad issued Royal Decree No. 35, amending some provisions of the Workers Trade Union Law. Labor Minister Jameel Humaidan said the amendment would enable more federations "to defend the interests [of workers] and it will prevent union monopoly that could be exercised if there is only one union in the establishment."[322] The Chamber of Deputies approved the amendment on January 31, 2012, and the Shura Council passed it on March 26, 2012. Under the new provisions, two or more trade unions in similar industry can establish a trade union federation if the majority members of general assemblies of the two unions approve. The decree prohibits establishing unions on religious and ethnic bases.

Bahraini authorities had a different position prior to the events of February and March 2011. In its Universal Periodic Submission to the UN Human Rights Council in 2008, the government argued that "trade union pluralism can weaken and split the trade union movement," and that "all States tend to place restrictions on pluralism and limit the number of trade unions and federations, placing them under the umbrella of a single entity so they can address economic challenges."[323]

In the context of government accusations that the GFBTU was effectively a wing of the opposition, it appeared that the authorities intended the new decree to weaken the GFTBU. A union leader put it this way:

---

[320] See: US Department of Labor, "Public report of review of U.S. submission 2011-01 (Bahrain)", December 20, 2012, http://www.dol.gov/ilab/programs/otla/20121220Bahrain.pdf (accessed January 17, 2013).

[321]" U.S. requests talks with Bahrain over 2011 labor crackdown,"Reuters, May 7, 3013, http://www.reuters.com/article/2013/05/07/us-usa-bahrain-labor-idUSBRE94615220130507 (accessed May 28, 2013).

[322] "Minister of Labour: Amendments to the Workers Trade Union Law are in line with international standards (وزير العمل:) تعديلات قانون النقابات منسجمة مع المعايير الدولية)," Al-Wasat, October 10, 2011, http://www.alwasatnews.com/3320/news/read/600260/1.html (accessed June 26, 2012)

[323] "Universal Periodic Review of the State of Bahrain,"Human Rights Watch, April 7, 2008, http://www.hrw.org/news/2008/04/06/universal-periodic-review-state-bahrain.

In principle trade union pluralism is welcome and it is good when it is for the interest of the workers. However I fear that the purpose of this amendment is to serve a blow to the [GFBTU] by paving the way to create a trade union federation that is pro-government.[324]

The Brussels-based International Trade Union Confederation expressed concern that the new amendment might be used to cancel registrations of "existing trade unions by falsely claiming that they were formed on sectarian lines."[325]

In a letter to the Shura Council on February 16, 2012, the GFBTU urged rejection of the amendment:

In terms of timing this amendment came in the wake of targeting the trade unions and [aims] to fragment the unity between the trade unions....This [amendment] should have been a subject of consultation between the government, represented by the Ministry of Labor, and workers, represented by the GFBTU.[326]

The new amendment also grants the minister of labor the power to decide which trade union confederation will represent Bahrain in international meetings and events, and engage in collective bargaining at the national level.[327] The GFBTU also rejected these provisions, saying that the federation representing the majority of workers should represent the country and engage in collective bargaining.

The amendment bans anyone found guilty of violating any law from holding trade union office for five years. The GFBTU considered this an "explicit intervention" in the affairs of

---

[324] Human Rights Watch Skype interview with a union leader (name withheld), August 6, 2012.

[325] "2012 Annual Survey of Violations of Trade Unions Rights-Bahrain," International Trade Union Confederation, June 6, 2012 http://www.unhcr.org/refworld/publisher,ITUC,,BHR,4fd889662,0.html (accessed June 20, 2012).

[326] "The position of the General Federation of Bahrain Trade Union in regard to Decree No. 35 of 2011 to amend the law of Unions, (موقف الاتحاد العام لنقابات عمال البحرين من المرسوم بقانون رقم 35 لسنة 2011 بتعديل قانون النقابات)," Shura Council, http://www.shura.bh/Council/Sessions/ShuraCouncil/LT3/CP2/s23/Documents/08.pdf (accessed August 4, 2012).

[327] "His Majesty issues decrees," Bahrain News Agency, October 9, 2011, http://www.bna.bh/portal/en/news/475817 (accessed June 25, 2012). On June 2, 2013, the Cabinet amended article 8 of the Trade Union Law to add that the Minister of Labor should get approval from the Council of Ministers before deciding which workers' unions will represent Bahrain in international trade union gatherings. See: " Premier Chairs Cabinet Meeting, Bahrain News Agency, June 2, 2013, http://bna.bh/portal/en/news/563600 (accessed June 3, 2013).

trade unions and argued that only the unions' general assembly should have the right to discipline its members.[328]

In a June 2011 complaint filed with the ILO, the GFTBU said it feared that authorities might use the amendment to oust trade union leaders who participated in the protests of February and March 2011.[329] According to the GFTBU, 65 unionists were among those fired by private and public firms following the February and March demonstrations.[330] As of June 10, 2013, the private and public companies had not reinstated 17 of the dismissed unionists.[331] Some trade union leaders told Human Rights Watch that in the wake of crushing the demonstrations, authorities did not bring charges against them for "inciting illegal demonstrations." One union leader told Human Rights Watch that authorities have told him that his case has been "shelved," but that "they can revisit the case at any time."[332]

In June 2012, the ILO's Committee on Freedom of Association called on Bahrain to amend this provision of the king's decree which bans anyone found guilty of violating any law from holding trade union office for five years and "in the meantime, confirm that this provision cannot be used for convictions relating to the exercise of legitimate trade union activity or the exercise of the right to peaceably demonstrate."[333]

Soon after the amendment became effective in March 2012, at least 10 new trade unions and one new trade union federation quickly emerged.[334] On July 18, six trade unions that had withdrawn from the GFBTU, accusing it of becoming a political tool of the opposition,

---

[328] The position of the General Federation of Bahrain Trade Union in regard to Decree No. 35 of 2011 to amend the law of Unions, (موقف الاتحاد العام لنقابات عمال البحرين من المرسوم بقانون رقم 35 لسنة 2011 بتعديل قانون النقابات), Shura Council, http://www.shura.bh/Council/Sessions/ShuraCouncil/LT3/CP2/s23/Documents/08.pdf (accessed August 4, 2012).

[329] International Labour Organization, Committee on Freedom of Association, Complaint against the Government of Bahrain presented by the International Trade Union Confederation (ITUC), Report No. 364, Case No. 2882 (2012), paras. 232-308. http://www.ilo.org/wcmsp5/groups/public/---ed_norm/---relconf/documents/meetingdocument/wcms_183430.pdf (accessed July 15, 2012).

[330] Human Rights Watch email correspondence with Karim Radhi, November 1, 2012.

[331] Human Rights Watch email correspondence with General Federation of Bahrain Trade Unions provided the figure to Human Rights Watch, June 10, 2013

[332] Human Rights Watch Skype interview with a union leader (name withheld), August 6, 2012.

[333] International Labour Organization, Committee on Freedom of Association, Complaint against the Government of Bahrain presented by the International Trade Union Confederation (ITUC), Report No. 364, Case No. 2882 (2012), para. 308 (i), http://www.ilo.org/wcmsp5/groups/public/---ed_norm/---relconf/documents/meetingdocument/wcms_183430.pdf (accessed July 15, 2012).

[334] Human Rights Watch interview with Salman al-Mahfoodh, secretary general of GFBTU, Manama, February 28, 2013. The number of newly established trade unions is based on media reports compiled by Human Rights Watch.

established the Bahrain Free Labour Unions Federation (BFLUF). The six trade unions were from Aluminum Bahrain (Alba), Bahrain Petroleum Company (Bapco), Bahrain Airport Services (BAS), Bankers Union, Gramco, and the Gulf Petrochemical Industries Co. (GPIC).[335] All are large firms in which the government holds substantial or even controlling interest.[336]

On July 31, 2012 the BFLUF accused the Ministry of Labor of "procrastination" for refusing to accept the documents that would officially establish the new trade federation. The same day, the prime minister issued a directive calling for "speeding up" measures to register the BFLUF.[337] One week later, the minister of labor met with the BFLUF board members to congratulate them on the establishment of the new federation.[338]

---

[335] "New breakaway union launched," *Gulf Daily News*, July 19, 2012 http://www.gulf-daily-news.com/NewsDetails.aspx?storyid=334302 (accessed July 20, 2012).

[336] Human Rights Watch Skype interview with a union leader (name withheld), February 26, 2013.

[337] "Prime Minister instructs the need for to speed up the completion of registering the Bahrain Free Labour Unions Federation (وزير العمل لنقابات الحر الاتحاد اشهار إجراءات إتمام لسرعة يوجه الوزراء رئيس)," *Al-Watan*, July 31, 2012, http://www.alwatannews.net/NewsViewer.aspx?ID=R050_838__737_bjNnisqWatfxqeRw_939__939_&item=x (accessed August 6, 2012).

[338] "Minister of Labor receives executive members of the Bahrain Free Labour Unions Federation (التنفيذي المجلس يلتقي العمل وزير للاتحاد الحر لنقابات عمل البحرين)," *Al-Wasat*, August 6, 2012, http://www.alwasatnews.com/3621/news/read/692852/1.html (accessed August 6, 2012).

V. Recommendations

To the National Assembly and the Government of Bahrain

On the Draft Law on Civil Organizations and Institutions

- Release of all individuals in Bahrain who have been imprisoned solely for exercising their rights to freedom of expression, association and assembly, including leaders of opposition political societies and NGOs.
- Amend article 2 to eliminate restrictions on establishing NGOs on "a factional or sectarian basis or to achieve objectives contrary to the provisions of the constitution or legislation in force in the Kingdom of Bahrain, or the public order and morals, or [if their] activities include engaging in politics";
- Specify that any language on "public order or morals" should be interpreted in a narrow and proportionate fashion, in conformity with article 22 of the International Covenant on Civil and Political Rights and the authoritative commentary of the UN Human Rights Committee.
- Amend article 3 to reduce the required number of founders.
- Amend article 6 to eliminate the requirement to provide a two-year budget when applying for registration.
- Remove article 7, which prohibits a member of one NGO to become a member of another NGO if the organizations conduct similar activities unless approved by the Minister of Social Development.
- Amend article 8 to indicate that the absence of a Ministry of Social Development response to a request for registering civic organizations within 60 days signifies approval; require the Ministry of Social Development to provide a written statement detailing reasons for rejecting any NGO application and ensure that the NGO has an opportunity to correct any defects in its application.
- Amend article 16 to remove restrictions on conditions for affiliating or collaborating with foreign NGOs.
- Permit NGOs to engage in any fundraising activity including public campaigns unless specifically prohibited by law. Do not require permission to engage in specific actions on fundraising, and require at most annual or bi-annual reporting.

- Amend article 17 to permit receipt of donations or transfers from foreign donors without government's approval, as long as all regulations regarding transparency and customs declarations for monetary transfers are met.
- Amend article 20 and 27 to eliminate the authority of the Ministry of Social Development to:
    - Appoint a temporary board of management to NGOs; and
    - Attend board meetings and require notifications of meetings.
- Amend article 22 to eliminate the Ministry of Social Development's authority to merge NGOs "if they work to achieve similar objectives... or to modify their purposes depending on the needs of the society... or for other reasons." The law should allow rather than force NGOs to merge.
- Amend article 58 to eliminate the Ministry of Social Development's authority to temporarily shut down NGOs and ensure that temporary closures occur only by judicial order and in response to serious violations of the law and;
- Guarantee the right of temporarily closed NGOs to rectify the violation and appeal the closure.
- Amend article 87 (1) of the draft law and article 163 of the Penal Code to abolish fines and prison terms for conducting peaceful and noncriminal activities on behalf of unregistered as well as registered NGOs.
- Amend article 87 (9) to abolish fines and prison terms for inviting foreigners to visit Bahrain for activities such as conferences and forums without prior permission from relevant authorities.

On Political Societies

- Amend article 4 (4) of the Political Societies law (No. 26/2005) to eliminate restrictions on establishing political society "class, sect, geography, profession, religion, language, race or sex" bases.
- Amend article 5 to reduce the minimum age for membership in political societies from 21 to 18.
- Amend article 22 to remove suspending political societies for 30 days while pending trial for violating Bahraini laws by;
    - Making clear that temporary closures occur only by judicial order and in response to serious violations of the law; and

o   Guaranteeing the right of temporarily closed political societies to rectify the violation and to appeal the closure.
- Implement the recommendation of the Bahraini Independent Commission of Inquiry which advised "relaxing censorship and allowing the opposition greater access to television broadcasts, radio broadcasts and print media."

On Trade Unions

- Respect the right of workers to establish and join the trade union(s) of their choice and peacefully assemble and associate with others without government interference.
- Amend the Workers Trade Union Law (Law 33/2002) to allow public sector workers to create and join trade unions.
- Ratify key International Labour Organization conventions including the Freedom of Association and Protection of the Right to Organise Convention, 1948 (No. 87), and the Right to Organise and Collective Bargaining Convention, 1949 (No. 98).

On the United Nations Special Rapporteur

- Respond positively to the requests of the United Nations special rapporteurs on torture, the rights to freedom of peaceful assembly and of association and the situation of human rights defenders to visit Bahrain.

To Member States of the United Nations Human Rights Council

- Adopt a resolution at the 24th session of the Human Rights Council in September 2013 that: expresses concern about the situation of human rights in Bahrain and the government's lack of cooperation with Special Procedures of the Human Rights Council; calls for the implementation of the recommendations of the Bahrain International Commission of Inquiry (BICI) and for Bahrain to swiftly facilitate access to Special Procedures and to engage with the Office of the High Commissioner for Human Rights (OHCHR); and asks the OHCHR to report back on the implementation of these requests.

To the United States

- Actively and publicly press for the immediate and unconditional release of all individuals in Bahrain who have been imprisoned solely for exercising their rights to freedom of expression, association and assembly, including leaders of political societies and NGOs.[339]

- Publicly urge Bahraini authorities to revise the Draft Law on Civil Organizations and Institutions and amend the Political Societies Law and the Workers Trade Union Law to bring the legislation into line with international standards in order to allow for freedom of association, expression and peaceful assembly.
- Speak out against Bahrain's intimidation and harassment of civil society organizations and activists. Conduct an assessment of the Bahraini government's steps to uphold the rights to freedom of assembly, expression, and association under international law and publicize the findings.
- Step up strategic and public contacts with Bahraini civil society in Bahrain and abroad.
- Call on Bahraini authorities to cooperate with and grant immediate access to the United Nations special rapporteurs on torture, freedom of assembly and association, and human rights defenders.
- Urge Bahrain to sign a Memorandum of Understanding with the Office of the High Commissioner on Human Rights (OHCHR) to establish an office in Bahrain with a mandate to assist, monitor and report on human rights developments.
- Seek a dedicated UN Human Rights Council (HRC) debate about continued violations of basic human rights in Bahrain and support an HRC resolution requesting that the UN High Commissioner for Human Rights keep the Council informed about Bahrain's progress in release of prisoners, accountability for crimes and legal reforms.

To the member states of the European Union

In line with commitments made in the EU Strategic Framework on Human Rights and Democracy, the European Union (including EU Member States, European EAS, European Commission, and European Parliament) should:

Protest leaders currently in prison: Abd al-Hadi al-Khawaja (also a citizen of Denmark), Abd al-Wahab Hussein, Hassan Ali Mushaima, Muhammad al-Muqdad (also a citizen of Sweden), Abd al-Jalil al-Muqdad, Abduljalil al-Singace, Seed al-Nuri, Abd al-Hadi al-Mukhudar, Mirza al-Mahrus, Muhammad Ali Rida Ismail, Muhammad Jawwad Muhammad, Ibrahim Sharif, Salah al-Khawaja, Nabeel Rajab, Zainab al-Khawaja (also a citizen of Denmark).

- Actively and publicly press for the immediate and unconditional release of all individuals in Bahrain who have been imprisoned solely for exercising their rights to freedom of expression, association and assembly, including leaders of political societies and NGOs, some of whom are dual citizens of Bahrain and EU member states.
- Publicly urge Bahraini authorities to revise the Draft Law on Civil Organizations and Institutions and amend the Political Societies Law on Political Societies and the Workers Trade Union Law to bring the legislation into line with international standards in order to allow for freedom of association, expression, and peaceful assembly.
- Speak out against Bahrain's intimidation and harassment of civil society organizations and activists. Conduct an assessment of the Bahraini government's steps to uphold the rights to freedom of assembly, expression, and association under international law and publicize the findings.
- Step up strategic and public contacts with Bahraini civil society in Bahrain and abroad.
- Call on Bahraini authorities to cooperate with and grant immediate access to the United Nations special rapporteurs on torture, freedom of assembly and association, and human rights defenders.
- Urge Bahrain to sign a Memorandum of Understanding with the Office of the High Commissioner on Human Rights to establish an office in Bahrain with a mandate to assist, monitor and report on human rights developments.
- Seek a dedicated UN Human Rights Council (HRC) debate about continued violations of basic human rights in Bahrain and support an HRC resolution requesting that the UN High Commissioner for Human Rights keep the Council informed about Bahrain's progress in release of prisoners, accountability for crimes and legal reforms.

Acknowledgements

Mariwan R. Hama, Arthur Koenig Fellow at Human Rights Watch, researched and wrote this report. Joe Stork, deputy director at Human Rights Watch's Middle East and North Africa Division, and Danielle Haas, senior editor in the Program Office, edited the report. Clive Baldwin, senior legal advisor, provided legal review. A Bahraini lawyer who preferred not to be named also reviewed the report. Researcher Faraz Sanei and Salma Abdou and Shannon Mich, interns with the Middle East and North Africa Division, provided research assistance. Amr Khairy, Arabic translation and website coordinator with the Middle East and North Africa division, supervised translation of this report into Arabic. Grace Choi, publications director, and Fitzroy Hepkins, mail manager, prepared the report for publication.

Human Rights Watch thanks Sayed Mohsin al-Alawi from the Bahraini Lawyers' Society, Sayed Yusuf al-Muhafadha of the Bahrain Center for Human Rights, Muhammad al-Maskati of the Bahrain Youth Society for Human Rights, Jalila Salman, vice president of the Bahraini Teachers' Society and Matar Matar and Jawad Fairooz from Al Wefaq Society for sharing their experience with us and their invaluable assistance during the research phase for this of this report.

Appendix: Letter from Human Rights Watch to Minister of Social Development Dr. Fatima Al-Balooshi, May 13, 2013

May 13, 2013

Dr. Fatima Al-Balooshi
Minister of Human Rights and Social Development
Kingdom of Bahrain

Your Excellency,

I am writing to request information regarding the legal restrictions faced by non-governmental organizations (NGOs) in Bahrain. Human Rights Watch has conducted research on this topic during trips to Bahrain in 2011 and in February 2013, when we met with members of civil society and the Ministry of Social Development. On the basis of this research, we are preparing a report that sets out our conclusions and concerns.

Our findings indicate that your government's restrictive approach to Bahraini NGOs violate international standards by: arbitrarily rejecting registration applications and imposing intrusive governmental supervision of NGOs; taking over and in some cases dissolving organizations whose leaders have criticized government officials or their policies; and placing substantial limits on the ability of groups to fund raise and receive foreign funding. While the current NGO law guarantees the freedom to establish associations, our findings indicate that in practice the authorities have used the loosely worded provisions of the law to significantly narrow the scope for establishing and operating civic organizations and restrict their capacity to function.

We would appreciate responses from your office to the questions below by May 31, 2013 in order to be able to reflect your government's perspective in our report and in our public comments when releasing the report. We plan to release the report in Bahrain on June 20, 2013.

The following questions relate to the current Law of Associations, Social and Cultural Clubs, Special Committees Working in the Field of Youth and Sports, and Private Institutions (Law of Associations No. 21/1989) and its implementation in practice by the authorities.

Denial of Registration

We understand that registration of NGOs is mandatory under the Law of Associations, and that under article 11 an application is considered rejected if the ministry does not respond within 60 days.

Human Rights Watch is aware of other cases where registration was denied on different grounds. The Ministry of Social Development in 2005 refused to register the Bahrain Youth Society for Human Rights (BYSHR). According to the US State Department, the Ministry of Social Development rejected BYSHR's registration application "allegedly because of its ties to the dissolved Bahrain Center for Human Rights (BCHR) and because some of its members were younger than the 18 [years old]." One of the group's founders told Human Rights Watch that he was the youngest among the founders and that he was 18 when the group applied for registration.

We understand that applicants are allowed to challenge the ministry's decision to reject an application at court, but that under article 12 (2) the court reviews officials' compliance with the formalities of registration under the Law of Association and tests whether the officials properly used their authority to deny a registration. We understand that the current Law of Associations does not require authorities to notify NGOs when they reject an application to register.

1) How many NGOs have applied for registration and whose registration has been denied? We would appreciate if you could provide us with a list of the organizations that have attempted to register since the Ministry of Social Development took charge of managing NGOs in 2005 but have been denied permission or ruled ineligible, including specific reasons for the refusal in each case.

2) In cases where NGOs' registration applications have been denied, and the applicants challenged the denial in court, we would appreciate if you could provide, in each case, the name of the organization, and the courts' decision on its challenge, or the current status of its challenge before the courts?

3) Have the authorities notified any applicants whose requests to register NGOs were rejected? If so, how many, and did the notifications include a reasoned explanation for the denial or rejection of the application?

4) Have the authorities reconsidered the application of BYSHR to register as an NGO? If so, when, and what was the result? Which member(s) of the group were younger than 18 at the time it initially sought to register?

Prohibited Activities, Imposition of Control and Dissolution

Our findings indicate that registered NGOs are subject to overbroad prohibitions on their activities and are vulnerable to government takeover or arbitrary dissolution. Article 18 of the Law of Associations says that organizations "may not get involved in politics." Under articles 23, 47, and 50 of the Law of Associations, the Ministry of Social Development can appoint ministry officials to take over NGOs for up to one year, cancel results of elections, and permanently dissolve or temporarily close organizations if the group is "unable to achieve its aims." Article 50 says that authorities can dissolve NGOs if they think the NGOs are "unable to achieve the aims [they were] established for... or if they violate the association law, public order and norms."

For instance, in September 2010, the Ministry of Social Development dissolved the board of directors of the Bahrain Human Rights Society (BHRS) and replaced its president with a ministry official because, according to a ministry statement on September 1, 2010, it was "serving a certain segment of the citizens." A few days earlier, in a press conference on August 28, the BHRS's director had criticized the government's denial of basic rights to detainees arrested in August 2010, and had said that the arrests amounted to "enforced disappearance."

1) What procedures does the ministry use to determine when an organization's activities violate article 18 of the Law of Associations? In particular, how does the ministry decide if an organization's activities are "political?"

2) In each case where NGOs have been found to be unlawfully participating in "politics," we would appreciate if you could provide the name of the NGO, the specific banned activity it engaged in, the specific penalty that was imposed, and the date.

3) How does the ministry determine if an NGO is "unable to achieve" its "aims" or "objectives," or violates relevant laws? In each case where the authorities have

dissolved an NGO on these bases, please provide the name of the NGO, the prohibited activity it engaged in, whether it was dissolved temporarily or permanently, the duration of the temporary dissolution (where appropriate), and the date it was dissolved.

4) In each case since 2005 where the ministry has appointed ministry officials to take over an NGO's board, please provide the name of the NGO, the number of board members and directors that the ministry assigned to it, and the justification for taking control of the board.

5) In each case where the ministry has cancelled the results of an NGO's internal elections, please provide the name of the NGO, the date of the election result that was cancelled, and the reasons for which the ministry cancelled their elections.

Limitations on Fundraising

Our research indicates that while Bahraini laws and regulations do not prohibit fundraising activities, they significantly curtail soliciting and receiving domestic and foreign funds. Article 21 of the Law of Associations prohibits any types of fundraising without written permission from authorities. According to a January 2006 Ministry of Social Development Decree (No. 27) NGOs must inform the ministry how they will collect money, the name and number of the bank account, and how they will spend the funds. If the ministry does not respond favorably within 30 days, the request is considered denied. Under article 9 of the decree, associations must record the name of every donor, eliminating any chance for anonymous donations. Article 14 of the Ministerial Decree grants the ministry power to "confiscate [funds] and distribute [them] to social activities" it favors if it considers the organization in question to have violated conditions laid out by the ministry in the fundraising license.

1) How many fundraising requests has the ministry rejected since 2005? We would appreciate if you could provide us with a list of those organizations whose requests have been denied, including specific reasons for the refusal in each case.

2) Has the ministry imposed any administrative or disciplinary measures on any organization for having received funds from abroad without permission? If so, in each case, please provide the name of the organization, the measures imposed against it, including the amount of funding confiscated or assets frozen, and the reasons for imposing these measures under the law.

3) Has the ministry imposed any administrative or disciplinary measures on any organization for having collected funds from local sources without permission? If so, in each case, please provide the name of the organization, the measures imposed against it, including the amount of funding confiscated or assets frozen, and the reasons for imposing these measures under the law.

Draft Law of Association

On August 12, 2012, the Bahrain News Agency reported that the Council of Ministers had adopted a draft NGO law.

Our research indicates that authorities did not consult civil society organizations ahead of adopting the legislation and that civic organizations were not aware of its adoption until media reported it. On August 15, 2012 Najwa Janahi, director of NGO affairs in the Ministry of Social Development, claimed that the government had consulted with representatives of civic organizations and experts in 2007.

We are concerned that the draft law passed by the Council of Ministers in 2012 and submitted to the National Assembly in January 2013 appears more restrictive than the 2007 draft, and in some respect more restrictive than the 1989 law currently in place.

For example, article 2 of the new draft law would allow the authorities to prohibit establishing NGOs for reasons that appear excessively broad and vague, such as "to achieve objectives contrary to the provisions of the constitution or legislation in force in the Kingdom of Bahrain, or the public order and morals, or [if their] activities include engaging in politics."

Under article 8 the Ministry of Social Development would be able to reject the registration of an NGO if it determines that "[Bahraini] society does not need its services… or if [the NGO was founded] in order to revive another NGO that was dissolved or merged into another organization."

Other restrictions in the draft law appear unduly restrictive and in some cases to lack any clear relationship to reasonable oversight requirements. For instance, article 6 would require an organization seeking to register to have a "two-year operational budget" and to provide evidence that it has a physical office.

According to article 7 a member of one NGO would not be able to join another NGO if the two organizations "conduct similar activities, unless approved by the minister." Under article 88 of the draft law NGOs would also need prior permission from "the minister [of social development] and relevant authorities" to invite foreigners to visit Bahrain for activities such as conferences and forums.

Under article 17 NGOs would be able to accept donations and raise funds only after receiving "written permission" from the Ministry of Social Development and in accordance with the executive regulations of the law.

Finally, article 58 would allow the ministry to close any organization that it determines to have committed violations, and to seek its permanent dissolution within 60 days by administrative court order. The article also says that the "order shall be implemented by force if necessary."

1. What are the specific steps the ministry took in order to consult with stakeholders, especially civil society organizations, before adopting the draft law of associations?
2. What are the criteria that the government would use to determine whether an NGO's proposed activities are against "public order and morals" or would constitute engaging in politics, such that the NGO's request to register would be denied under article 2?
3. What are the criteria that the government would use to determine that an NGO's services are not needed by Bahraini society such that the NGO's request to register would be denied under article 8?
4. Please explain the rationale or need for the following provisions:
    a. The provision of article 8 that would deny registration to an NGO that the government deems to have been dissolved or that merged into another NGO?
    b. The provision of article 6 that would prohibit a member of one NGO from joining another NGO that conducts similar activities, without prior approval?
    c. The provision of article 88 requiring prior approval for NGOs to invite foreigners to events?
5. Article 17 of the draft law says that NGOs would be able to raise funds after receiving "written permission" from your ministry and in accordance with executive

regulations. Can you tell us whether or not Decree No. 27 of 2006 will remain in force if the draft law is approved by the parliament and signed into law by the King?

6. What due process guarantees, if any, do NGOs have if the minister decides to close them? Can they, for example, challenge such a ministerial decision and continue operating, prior to being closed for up to 60 days before the minister needs to seek a court order for their permanent dissolution under article 58?

In order to be able to reflect your responses in our report, we look forward to receiving them by May 31, 2013. We also reiterate our interest in arranging a meeting to discuss these issues in person.

Thank you for your consideration.

Sincerely,

Sarah Leah Whitson
Executive Director
Middle East and North Africa Division
Human Rights Watch